I0212195

Thrive

IN TRUE IDENTITY

31 Days

for women to be
empowHERed
by the Word

DR. CRYSTAL CLAY

DrCrystalClay. © 2020

All rights reserved. No part of this book may be reproduced, stored, or transmitted by any means- whether auditory, graphic, mechanical, or electronic-without written permission of both publisher and author, except in the case of brief excerpts used in critical articles and certain other noncommercial uses permitted by copyright law. Unauthorized reproduction of any part of this work is illegal and is punishable by law.

ISBN: 978_0_947482_01_5

Because of the dynamic nature of the internet, any web addresses or links contained in this book may have changed since publication and may no longer be valid. The views expressed in this work are solely those of the author and do not necessarily reflect the views of the publisher, and the publisher disclaims any responsibility for them.

Printed in the United States of America

www.olivebranch.bm

Unless otherwise indicated, Scripture is taken from the New King James Version of the Bible.

To my two gifts, Bianca and Courtney,
and all daughters around the world...
Thrive in Your True Identity!

Hello Powfterful Friend,

Thank you for joining me on this journey to rediscover you in a new and fresh way: the way in which God originally intended. God wants you to know the truth about who you are, who He designed you to be; who you are called to be. His desire is for you to live an abundant life, one where you can be free; free to "Be…" You can finish the sentence with whatever speaks to your life.

The journey to freedom is not easy. When we were children, it seemed as though we were fearless, saw life as limitless. We were hopeful and optimistic about our future. As we face some of life's harsh realities however, that courageous spirit, those limitless possibilities, dreams, and visions seem to grow dimmer and dimmer. It is as though one day we woke up and found ourselves in a place where we have lost our identity. We somehow became a shadow of ourselves, surviving through life rather than thriving in life.

How do I know this? Because that is my story. This devotional spoke to me first as I sought the Lord daily on a journey to rediscover who I truly was; not what the world expected of me or thought of me, or not even who I thought I should be, rather who God made me to be.

I speak of a journey because I am still on a journey. I don't believe I will fully arrive until the Lord calls me home, but my aim is to live this life on purpose, with intentionality, harnessing my voice, leveraging my gifts, pushing others forward, pulling others up, speaking life to dark places and giving others hope. My passion is that all women will see themselves as God sees them.

When we see ourselves as God sees us, it changes everything. God is the Chief Architect and He has the blueprint. When we follow His blueprint for our lives, it is no longer a struggle. We do not have to compete or compare. We only must follow the unique design God created for our lives.

This devotional was not my original vision. The Lord woke me up one Saturday morning and told me to start a 31-day bible study called 'Thrive in True Identity'. The theme was familiar to me as three years prior, God gave me the vision when I had the honor of leading a women's season at my church. That Saturday morning, I immediately began to write the vision as God laid it on my heart. God truly did the rest.

The next 31 days consisted of an intimate walk with God trusting Him for fresh manna daily as I waited on His inspired word and biblical principles that strengthened my spiritual walk, helped to navigate relationships, supported personal and professional growth and shifted negative mindsets. I took great joy in sharing these key lessons with a group of amazing ladies around the world; many who encouraged me to write this book. For this I am profoundly grateful.

My prayer is that as you turn the pages of this devotional, you will meet with God in a new and fresh way. As I share my stories, I pray that God will remind you of your stories, make your journey 'crystal clear', give you insight into your past, revelation of your present and hope for your future. As you lean into God to hear His voice, may He open your eyes to allow you to see the real you. I then challenge you to show up as the real you boldly, fearlessly, embracing who you are in Him.

Now let the journey begin! We will start with knowing and growing in Christ. We will then embrace the process of glowing in Christ as He transforms our thinking and renews our mindsets. That is not however where the journey ends.

We then have a responsibility once we are on the "glow up" to "show up" for ourselves and others. Once we have fully experienced the hand of God on our lives, we can then begin to PowHer Up by lifting others up and bringing them along in the journey.

You are God's masterpiece, a unique treasure. You were born to thrive. This is your 31-day challenge for you to 'Thrive in your True Identity'!

Rich Blessings,

Crystal

"...I have come that they may have life, and that they may have it more abundantly." John 10:10

Table of Contents

PART

1

Knowing

But you are a chosen generation, a royal priesthood, a holy nation, His own special people, that you may proclaim the praises of Him who called you out of darkness into His marvelous light.

1 Peter 2:9

Who are you? This understanding is one of the most significant issues people grapple with, and yet the answer to this question is a key determinant of many of our life's decisions and ultimately our quality of life. Many times I thought I knew my identity, but when adverse circumstances struck, I temporarily forgot and made temporary decisions with long-term, unintended consequences.

Social media has its benefits, but it also has taken a toll on many people's identity. The images we see on social media change the way we think about ourselves. Young people especially are often negatively impacted by the images and values portrayed on social media, sadly at a time when their identity is being formed in their teenage years. If not addressed at this critical stage, it trickles into self-limiting beliefs in later years. Temporary decisions with far-reaching, unseen consequences.

I recently asked a panel of women leaders, "What advice would you give to your twenty-year-old self?" Inevitably, the responses were all wrapped in wisdom related to things they would have done differently if they had a different perception of themselves, expectations of themselves, or placed a different value upon themselves. The underlying theme I saw throughout their responses is that the most significant transformational impact in a Christian's walk is to ground their identity in Christ.

How do you begin to understand how to ground your identity in Christ—the kind of grounding that is unshakeable and can always be recognized for its true value? In 2008, Louis Vuitton's (LV) new release was the LV Urban Satchel, described as one of a kind. It was also one of Louis Vuitton's most expensive bags. What is most interesting about this bag is that it was literally a pile of trash glued onto the carry on. The selling price however for that bag with the pile of trash was $150,000. Why would they sell for such a high price? Because as a company, Louis Vuitton was confident in their brand identity. The name speaks for itself.

If LV can be so confident in their name, as daughters of the most High God—whose name is above all names—if we are His own designer masterpiece, surely we can be confident in our identity in Christ. The more closely we are drawn to God, the more we discover our true identity.

When we begin to see God's perspective and value of us and embrace the revelation that we are a chosen people, a royal priesthood, God's very own possession, everything changes!

1. What advice would you give to your younger self about the importance of knowing your identity?

_____

_____

_____

_____

_____

_____

_____

_____

_____

2. How does that advice apply to you now?

_____

_____

_____

_____

_____

_____

_____

_____

_____

_____

NOTES:

DAY 2: IT'S TIME TO LIVE UP TO YOUR NAME

As it is written: "For Your sake we are killed all day long; We are accounted as sheep for the slaughter." Yet in all these things we are more than conquerors through Him who loved us.

Romans 8:36–37 NKJV

In 1964, Blue Ribbon Sports initially served as an American distributor of running shoes made by a Japanese company. In 1971, Blue Ribbon Sports launched an effort to manufacture and distribute their own shoes—under their own brand. The story is told that the first shipment of their own shoes would go out the next day, and they needed a new name. With a deadline approaching of 9:00 a.m. and having few options, they chose the name *Nike,* which means *victorious* in Greek language, culture, and mythology.

In 2015, one company outpaced all other Dow Jones with a 30 percent gain: Nike. The Oregon-based $100 billion company started generating over $30 billion in yearly revenues, experiencing year-over-year growth of 5%, with sales to China growing more than 30% annually. Nike became the most popular and respected brand in the sports industry—and one of the most valued business brands in the world. Nike became victorious. Nike lived up to its name. You can also live up to your name!

As a Gallup Strengths coach, I implement a three-step exercise to help my clients begin to own their strengths and walk out their full potential.

1. **Name It:** The Greek word used for "we are more than conquerors" here is a single word, *hypernicōmen,* an inflected form of *hypernicaō.* The verb is composed of the basic verb, *nicaō,* (*conquer*) with the prefix *hyper-* (*over, beyond*) added to it. Part of the meaning of *supernikao* is the completeness of the victory. In other words, *supernikao* means "more than" and "to conquer overwhelmingly." For you this means *absolute* conquest. We are not just defeating tribulation, like a boxer who knocks down his opponent and he gets back up. This defeat will be overwhelming and final. **We are more than a conqueror,** which means "to be greater than a conqueror."

2. **Claim It:** Imagine buying a gift for someone, yet they won't receive it from you. They miss out on a gift that could be a tremendous blessing and might be just the thing they needed, but they would never know because they didn't take the time to claim it. In this case, to *claim it* means to appreciating the unique power and value you have and bring to others. Because God's plan for you is certain, you can face the most difficult circumstances with confidence. You don't merely *survive* your trials; you *thrive* as an overcomer because you're "more than a conqueror." He will make your enemies get up and serve you. He will make your enemies your footstool (Luke 20:43)

3. **Aim It:** *Supernikao* also refers to the size of the spoil—the amount of the prize. That prize—God's kingdom—is vast. But, that is still not all that Paul is trying to express by his use of *supernikao*. Aside from the totality of the victory and aside from the vastness of the prize, there is something else, something important, behind the meaning of *supernikao* as Paul uses it. That "something else" to Paul is to be more than a conqueror; to carry away the prize of victory without putting forth the effort, or take the risk, of a conqueror. That word *risk* is a key word. Risk is a significant part of any sacrifice. God, through Christ, risked everything when He made that sacrifice and became a human being. If there is no risk, there is no sacrifice; someone else does the fighting. One who is more than a conqueror shares in the prize without sharing in the lion's share of the risk of the struggle. Yes, we all struggle in part as Paul did; that is the human condition (John 16:13), but God fights the intensity of our battles for us (Exodus 14:14; 2 Chronicles 20:17). Those who are "more than conquerors" come along after the battle is won and enjoy the prize of victory. What does this mean for us? It means it's time to live up to our name!

We are already beneficiaries. Now we must be willing to do what God tells us to do! Follow the Nike slogan coined in 1988, "Just Do It"— Thrive in your true identity!

1. When you declare you are more than a conqueror, what is the evidence of that in your life?

_____

_____

_____

_____

_____

_____

_____

_____

2. What more do you need to Name It, Claim It, and Aim It to live up to your name?

_____

_____

_____

_____

_____

_____

_____

_____

_____

_____

"Eat your words!" Cassius Clay (later known as Muhammad Ali) shouted to the newsmen covering the fight of his life after he had been declared the new heavyweight champion of the world. Only three of the forty-six sportswriters covering the fight had picked him to win.

Years ago, my friend Janita and I started a lunchtime Bible study for working women. We started with the *The Battlefield of the Mind* by Joyce Meyers, accompanied by the workbook. We intended for it to be an eight-week study.

An indication of the intensity of the fight? The study lasted for nearly three years.

The most difficult struggle in the battle isn't with others' perceptions of what our battles look like. It is our own perceptions—the battlefield of the mind. The opponents in the ring are typically "I am" versus "They say I am" or "What I say I am" versus "What I really believe I am."

Who do you think you are?

I attended an "I am" series event some years ago with a lineup of sought-after celebrities. The moderator asked one of the panelists, "Who are you?" On the spot, the panelist paused for a minute. Eventually, he responded, "I am energy." I thought about the question and what my response would have been.

Regarding that question, I have admittedly found myself sometimes calibrating in my mind who I think I am, who other people think I am, who I want to be…the list goes on. David fought lions and a giant and many other battles, but the battlefield of the mind was one of his hardest struggles. It is a struggle to change your thoughts and behaviors when your identity is tied up with who people say you are—and more importantly with who *you* say you are. It is the single fiercest fight of your life.

In Psalm 139, the psalmist comes from a place of vulnerability and transparency, and in a simple and succinct way, puts an end to all the confusion. He simply says, "Lord, You have searched me and known me" (vs 1). He then continues to write about the true essence of the great power of God and how, because of that great power, every word David says and everywhere David goes, God already knows. No matter what or where he tries to hide, he is exposed. God can see through imposter syndrome, doubts, feelings of inadequacy, and failures. God knows it all, so much so that David admits he cannot even comprehend it.

As with anyone who questions how something is made, wisdom says to read the manual and find out what the manufacturer or maker says. David stops trying to figure it all out on his own and yields to the greatness of his Creator and writes, "For You formed my inward parts; you covered me in my mother's womb. I will praise You, for I am fearfully and wonderfully made" (vs. 13–14). David moved from confusion to confidence in his identity in God.

When we think about all we know about ourselves, fear can arise. If we focus on what we know about ourselves from a human perspective—negative self-image, unworthiness, shame—we can easily become stuck. If you live in a small community like I do, it can be challenging to shift your perspective because people tend to remind you of who you used to be. I recall starting a new job and was excited to meet my coworkers. One lady said, "Yes, I know you! Wasn't your ex-boyfriend so-and-so (referring to my unwise decisions from my teenage years)." It stunned me for a minute, because her question took me back to who I used to be.

We know too much about ourselves and all our imperfections. It makes us afraid or ashamed to declare what is true. The enemy also knows the negativity we have declared over ourselves and like the news reporters at the boxing match, has determined we are not going to win. When we question our identity, we wonder why God made us the way He did, with all our seeming imperfections.

Why do you fear what He knows about you? The point is, He knows! David marvels in verses seventeen and eighteen, "How precious also are Your thoughts to me, O God! How great is the sum of them! If I should count them, they would be more in number than the sand; when I awake, I am still with You." God constantly thinks of us and is concerned about the details of our lives. It doesn't matter what we've done—He cares, because it's less about who you are and more about Who God is!

Who we are brings *fear*. Who He is brings *wonder*! We don't need to fear, for we know Who God is and we know He knows us. First John 4:18 says, "There is no fear in love; but perfect love casts out fear, because fear involves torment. But he who fears has not been made perfect in love."

Taking the "fear" off the battlefield allows you to live in the fullness of who God made you to be.

David saw God as a wonder, and at the end of Psalm 139 puts a stop to all the madness in the mind, all the questions, all the fear, all the wondering. Because of his words, we, like David, can acknowledge that His work is marvelous. When the enemy comes in like a flood and tries to make us question our identity or tries to take us back to who we used to be before God transformed our lives, in order to defeat us, we can tell the devil, "Eat your words! I am God's new heavyweight champion! I am fearfully and wonderfully made."

1. When you think about all you know about yourself, what provokes fear?

2. What does God say about you?

3. What do you need to do to fully embrace what God says about you?

August 1, 1834 is one of the most important dates in Bermuda's history. In my country, it marks the abolition of slavery and is one of our favorite public holidays. We call it Cup Match and we enjoy an exhilaratingly competitive cricket match, but more so, we celebrate the emancipation of slavery—we celebrate *freedom*. On that day, many people of color experienced a new level of freedom—freedom to earn, freedom to build, freedom to explore, freedom to provide.

We all know too well, however, that you can be "free" but still have a slave mentality, still be in bondage, still play victim, still be cast down, still feel entrapped. Like yesterday's message mentioned, there are real struggles that happen on the battlefield of your mind. Bob Marley penned *Redemption Song*, of which two lines always stand out to me, "Emancipate yourself from mental slavery, **none but ourselves can free our minds.**"

Those two lines remind me of Elijah, who experienced **great freedom**. He not only walked in his purpose, he walked with great power and authority. He knew who he was in God. He had utter confidence in the God he served as a prophet. He **declared a drought** and the brook dried up, until he said that it would rain. He **revived the widow's son**. He experienced a **major victory on Mount Carmel** when, after a simple prayer, the fire of the Lord fell and consumed a burnt sacrifice, forcing the Baal worshippers to say, "The Lord, He is God!" He **prophesied** to King Ahab that the **drought was going to end**, to prepare his chariot to escape the rain. In fact, Elijah even ran ahead of him. Elijah was not only free, he was extraordinarily *empowered*.

But something happened along the way. *Ahab told Jezebel all that Elijah had done.* And he didn't stop there. In 1 Kings 19:1, Ahab says, "also" (saving the best news for last) and tells Jezebel how Elijah executed all of the prophets of Baal. Jezebel, upon hearing this news, declared that Elijah would be dead within twenty-four hours. Suddenly, Prophet Elijah, mighty man of God, empowered to speak to kings, who had witnessed many miracles and God's hand at work in his life, and who sprinted toward victory, started running toward defeat.

One spoken word changed his course. Has that ever happened to you? Perhaps it wasn't one word, but one person, one friend, one manager, one pastor, one failure, one relationship, one disappointment, one opinion, one church member, one teacher. Someone said something that knocked you off your confident course.

I recall, during a peak time in my career, I was thriving and making an impact—until the organization restructured, and a new manager came on board. This person wanted power and complete control and they made sure to establish it that first day. While I adapted to the change, I didn't realize how much it impacted me until the CEO pulled me aside one day and said, "What's going on? We don't hear your voice anymore. We need to hear your voice. You have too much to offer. You don't need to shrink back." I'd allowed one person to push me to hide in the cave, just like Elijah. I was playing small.

Marianne Williamson described this phenomenon eloquently with these words: "We ask ourselves, 'Who am I to be brilliant, gorgeous, talented, fabulous?' Actually, who are you not to be? You are a child of God. Your playing small does not serve the world. There is nothing enlightened about shrinking so that other people won't feel insecure around you."[1]

Here's the good news: When one situation puts you in a cave, it only takes one voice to bring you out. The CEO gave me the awareness that I was "hiding in the cave" because of the new manager. Just as the Lord

---

[1] *A Return to Love: Reflections on the Principles of "A Course in Miracles"*

spoke to Elijah and said, "Go out, and stand on the mountain before the Lord" (vs. 11), God gave me the instruction to come out of my own cave and thrive again in my true identity.

Elijah allowed someone else to make him a prisoner and castaway, to encourage him to run from his calling. Has trouble moved you out of position, handcuffed you, made you shrink to a smaller version of yourself, no longer free to thrive in your true identity? Don't disqualify yourself from your position. Go and stand before the Lord!

Get into His presence and let God's plan unfold. God cares too much about you to leave you in the cave. He knows the truth anyway, so don't make excuses for why you are in the cave. Just as in verse 11, He will call to you and pass before you in His way when you honestly and vulnerably get into His presence.

Let God reposition you. He says to you like He said to Elijah in verse 15, "Go and return." He is speaking to you today in that still small voice and saying to you as He did to Elijah, "Go out (of the) cave (of depression, self-pity, fear, and the mindset that the giant is bigger than your God) and *stand*" (Emphasis and elaboration my own).

You have to be challenged to change!

"Won't you help to sing these songs of freedom? 'Cause all I ever have, redemption songs"

"God's Masterpiece"
Ephesians 2:10

REFLECTIONS:

1. Who or what is the Jezebel in your life that has pushed or is trying to push you into a cave?

_____

_____

_____

_____

_____

_____

_____

2. Is there something God has called you to do, but you got discouraged or feel you failed and walked away, gave up, threw in the tire, settled for less, and decided to play small?

_____

_____

_____

_____

_____

_____

_____

_____

DAY 5: STOLEN IDENTITY

For we are His workmanship, created in Christ Jesus for good works,
which God prepared beforehand that we should walk in them.
Ephesians 2:10 NKJV

Whenever we think of a masterpiece, we think of a work done with extraordinary skill by a master craftsman. When I think of a masterpiece, a great piece of artwork typically comes to mind. Masterpieces are such a marvelous phenomenon that they are sought after by not only master craftsmen, but masters of another—art thieves. FBI agents who specialize in busting art thieves find a common theme in the criminals they catch: art thieves steal masterpieces because they're priceless. The real quest in art theft is not in the stealing; it's in the selling.

One of my daughter's friends is a fashion designer whose designs were once stolen. At first, he did not even realized it happened. Curious, I wanted to know how, in the vast world of fashion design, he'd found out. My daughter told me a friend of the designer attended a fashion show in another city and recognized this gentleman's brand on the runway. His brand identity was so strong that his friend spotted it without intentionally looking for it. The thief knew the value of the workmanship, stole it, and tried to profit from it.

Satan does the same thing with us when he attempts to steal our identity. The first recorded incident of identity theft in the Bible is in Genesis 3. Satan used the serpent to trick Adam and Eve into believing God had selfish motives for not allowing them to eat from the Tree of the Knowledge of Good and Evil. His primary goal was to destroy the confidence that Adam and Eve had in their identity as children of the Most High God.

Satan is still using the same tactics today. His work comes in many different forms: domestic abuse, gaslighting, handing others power over you, letting others define or put labels on you, exposing you to constant criticism, people making you feel you don't belong, subconscious or conscious bias, and many more damaging methods. The enemy will do whatever it takes to diminish your value.

When I worked in human resources, I interviewed a senior executive who I knew from a previous workplace. I spoke well of him and was looking forward to having him showcase his talents and experience to the selection panel. The person I knew, however, did not show up for the interview; he was only a shadow of his true self. I was in disbelief, so much so that I called him later to find out what happened to him. What he described to me made me realize he had been beaten down so much at work that he forgot who he was. His identity was stolen.

Identity theft—in a worldly sense—is a tragedy. It makes a person feel so violated and vulnerable and puts their future at risk. People will go to all lengths to get their legal identity back. What if we took that same approach when others try to steal our identity in Christ?

You are God's masterpiece, His handiwork, a work of art, His unique design, His workmanship. He created you uniquely with extraordinary skill. That makes you a target of theft, not in the traditional sense of art theft, but in the sense of *identity theft*. The Bible says, "The thief does not come except to steal, and to kill, and to destroy" (John 10:10). The enemy, *the thief*, knows your worth and would not target you unless he was motivated to take something of significant value!

Step into the truth of who you are and show up as God's masterpiece. It's not who anyone else says you are that matters. *It's who God says you are.* Don't let other people define you. God has given you your identity. Own it. Boldly declare, "I am God's masterpiece!" and let that declaration govern how you show up today and every day.

I'll leave you with John 10:10 one more time: "The thief does not come except to steal, and to kill, and to destroy. I have come that they may have life, and that they may have it more abundantly."

1. How has God uniquely made you His masterpiece?

2. Has your identity been stolen?

3.   What do you need to do to get it back?

_____

_____

_____

_____

_____

_____

_____

_____

"God's Masterpiece"
Ephesians 2:10

DAY 6: CHOSEN

...just as He chose us in Him before the foundation of the world, that we should
be holy and without blame before Him in love, having predestined us to adoption
as sons by Jesus Christ to Himself, according to the good pleasure of His will...
Ephesians 1:4–5 NKJV

Recently, my husband and I had dinner with a friend we had not connected with for many years; I'll call him William. William spoke with such pride about his children and beamed when speaking of his daughter, who had just graduated and was heading to university. I admired his relationship with his daughter as he talked about how much their personalities were alike and that he couldn't wait to get home to beat her at an electronic game they had been playing.

Throughout the evening, I wracked my brain trying to remember this daughter, but I waited until dinner was over to tell my husband, "It's funny; I don't recall William having a daughter. I thought he only had a son. When did he have a daughter?"

"He adopted her a few years ago," my husband replied. I then realized there was no distinction in how William spoke about his son and his daughter. He seemed to love them equally. The only difference was that his son was born to him and his daughter was chosen by him.

The spirit of adoption is a powerful principle when we really take hold of it and apply it in our lives. Adoption involves a choice. The blessing of adoption is in the choosing and the being chosen. As children of God, we were chosen—we were *adopted*.

All believers are adopted in a spiritual sense. Jesus died so we could be adopted as children with the full rights and privileges as Christ's heirs. In the book of John, the apostle says, "But as many as received Him, to them He gave the right to become children of God, to those who believe in His name: who were born, not of blood, nor of the will of the flesh, nor of the will of man, but of God" (John 1:12–13 NKJV).

Ephesians 1:4 reinforces that verse, "We were chosen before the foundation of the world" (NKJV). We were set apart, especially created—as we found out yesterday in Ephesians 2:10—for the purposes of doing good work. It gave God great pleasure to choose us. It's a wonderful blessing to be chosen.

The heroine in the book of Esther was also adopted. Her uncle Mordecai adopted her as his own child. Esther may have lost twice, losing her two parents, but she also had the unique blessing of being chosen *three* times. First, she was chosen by Mordecai as a daughter. Second, Esther had the honor of being chosen by the king as his queen. Third, and most importantly, she was chosen to "do good work." Esther was chosen to save her people. In verse 14, we see Mordecai relaying a message to his niece, "For if you remain completely silent at this time, relief and deliverance will arise for the Jews from another place, but you and your father's house will perish. Yet who knows whether you have come to the kingdom for such a time as this?"

My mom died in her mid-fifties, and I recall her saying when she was sick, "I've only lived half my life." Because of this experience, I don't take life for granted. As I've come to the various ages and stages of my life, I've pause to reflect on the same question as Esther, "Why have I come to this place for such a time as this?" I'm still here for a reason. What is my "good work" in this season?

Esther knew her social identity—queen—but she only made a meaningful impact when she became an advocate for her people and thrived in her *true* identity.

Even people who have lived out their wildest dreams may still have doubts about their impact. Only God will ever know the full impact of our actions (Ecclesiastes 3:11 NKJV). The only way we can have any sense of satisfaction about our work here on Earth is when we know we have obeyed God and have done what He has called (or chosen) us to do.

Only you and God set the standard for what "thriving" means for you. It may look different from your sisters around you, so be careful to not compare, lest you fall off His track for you. If you stay focused on your true identity and your true calling, you're less likely to run the risk of getting stuck as an extra in someone else's movie, and never playing the leading role you were meant to fill.

Don't let your age or stage in life make you think it's too late or too early. "He has made everything beautiful in its time. Also He has put eternity in their hearts, except that no one can find out the work that God does from beginning to end" (Ecclesiastes 3:11 NKJV).

Who knows why you have been chosen for such a time as this!

"God's Masterpiece"
Ephesians 2:10

1. Have you done any good work?

2. What could your story be if you fully embraced the fact that you have been chosen for such a time as this?

DAY 7: KNOW YOUR WORTH

And at this point His disciples came, and they marveled that He talked with a woman; yet no one said, "What do You seek?" or, 'Why are You talking with her?' The woman then left her water pot, went her way into the city, and said to the men, "Come, see a Man who told me all things that I ever did."

John 4:27–28 NKJV

One of my favorite commonly referenced allegories is the story of the pocket watch. Here is one of my favorite versions of the story.

Before he died, a father said to his son, "Here is a watch that your grandfather gave me. It is almost two hundred years old. Before I give it to you, go to the jewelry store downtown. Tell them that I want to sell it, and see how much they offer you."

The son went to the jewelry store, came back to his father, and said, "They offered $150.00 because it's so old."

The father said, "Go to the pawnshop."

The son went to the pawnshop, came back to his father, and said, "The pawnshop offered $10.00 because it looks so worn."

The father asked his son to go to the museum and show them the watch. He went to the museum, came back, and said to his father, "The curator offered $500,000.00 for this very rare piece to be included in their precious antique collections."

The father said, "I wanted to let you know that the right place values you in the right way. Don't find yourself in the wrong place and get angry if you are not valued. Those that know your value are those who appreciate you, don't stay in a place where nobody sees your value."

Know your worth!

Women who know their worth:

1. **Don't** allow past mistakes to define them.

   The Samaritan woman came to the well feeling unworthy. She'd had five husbands and the one she was with at the time, was not her own, but Jesus accepted her just as she was. This does not mean He approved of her lifestyle, but He knew her worth. He knew where she was and what she needed. She came to the well with her head low and left with her head high. That's what happens when we have an encounter with Jesus and He reminds us of our true identity which rests in the fact that we are truly loved (Romans 5:8), completely forgiven, (Ephesians 1:7), and fully accepted (Romans 8:35–39)

   It's important to know your worth. It is equally important to acknowledge the worth of others. Accept people where they are. Do not judge people from *your* place of strength compared to *their* place of weakness.

2. **Don't** let others devalue them.

   When you know your worth, you don't let other people devalue you. One way people might try to define you is through abuse. An abusive friend, partner, spouse, or employer is unacceptable. Many are familiar with more common forms of abuse, like physical or sexual abuse. Less familiar are more subtle abuses that happen when people use mind games to control you and make you feel bad about yourself. Examples include extreme jealousy, monitoring social media, demanding passwords, blaming, shaming, isolating, intimidating, underpaying, unrealistic expectations, talking down to, and constant criticism are all forms of mental, emotional, workplace, and technological abuse and bullying.

   When you know better, you do better. If you are experiencing any of these types of abusive actions, you *can* stand strong in your identity in Christ and not allow these things to happen to you. Report it to HR if you are at work, remove yourself from the abusive situation, and, if necessary, report it to local authorities—especially if the abuse is physical.

3. **Stay away** from the "jewelry stores" and the "pawnshops."

   The most important value—if you'll allow me to coin another word—is to know your *valYou*! Women who know their worth avoid putting themselves in the wrong groups of friends, relationships, workplaces, or situations that compromise who they are, clip their wings, and limit their ability to fly.

   The jewelry stores and pawnshops will always try to devalue you and never acknowledge your worth. But you are a child of God and when your identity is solid in Him, you have no need for the jewelry stores and pawnshops. You don't even need to step inside.

"God's Masterpiece"
Ephesians 2:10

1. What past mistakes are you allowing to define you?

2. Who or what are the jewelry stores and pawnshops in your life? What do you need to do to remove them?

PART

2

Growing

DAY 8: IDENTITY CRISIS

I will make you exceedingly fruitful; and I will make nations of you,
and kings shall come from you.
Genesis 17:6 NKJV

The word *kaizen* is a Japanese term meaning "change for the better" and is often used in business as an attempt to create a culture of continuous improvement? The premise is that small incremental changes can make a big difference. However, the opposite is true of an identity crisis. One big change can have an endless amount of incremental changes in so many areas, and in so many lives, that it becomes vast over time.

All too frequently, we hear how someone we know well (or at least thought we did) did an "about-face" and become someone completely unrecognizable over time. One of the more common identity crises is a midlife crisis. This typically occurs between the ages of forty-five and fifty-five years old, due to a person's refusal to accept their advancing age or lack of accomplishments in life. Sadly, we see many marriages end because of this phenomenon when one of the partners suddenly runs off with someone in a different age bracket.

Adults, young and old, can also experience a social identity crisis. *Social Identity* is when people label themselves as part of a particular group. When an adult retires or is no longer part of an organization or position that holds status, he or she may experience an identity crisis. With teenagers, it's a little different and I would venture to say most parents can relate to the impact of the cruel social circle when one of their children comes home crying because "a friend" or "group of friends" decided to "unfriend" them. Today, it seems we have more low self-esteem, cyberbullying, and suicide watches in schools than ever before, mostly because of two words—identity crisis.

In Genesis, we see the ultimate excuse for someone to have an identity crisis in the story of Joseph. Joseph was favored by God and his father, but he was disregarded, dismissed, and sold by his brothers, whom he thought would protect him. He was falsely accused by his boss' wife and thrown in prison. He went from being the favored one to the forgotten one, but even in crisis, Joseph's identity was in God. The people who wronged Joseph stripped him of everything physical, but they could not strip him of his identity in God. The word of promise had already been spoken over him (Genesis 17:6).

There will always be attempts to shake your identity. That's why it is paramount to ground your identity in the one thing that cannot be shaken—the Word of God. Sadly, we spend so much of our time looking to the world for validation and to find our identity. We then find ourselves frustrated because we are still empty. Wealth, beauty, marital status, number of social media followers, power, career—all are shakable, and while they may provide some level of comfort, putting our faith in them is like building a house on sand. When the storms of life come, they can easily be blown away.

Do you want your identity to be unshakeable? Build your house on the rock. Jesus is the Rock, He's the firm foundation.

Your identity is in Christ, not the crisis! The word *crisis* originates from the Greek word *krisis*—which means "decisive moment." In one moment, in the middle of a crisis, everything can change, but we serve a God who does not change (Malachi 3:6).

1. Have you or someone you've known had an identity crisis? What was its impact on your life or their life?

2. Where are you looking for validation?

3. What "sand" do you need to remove to build your house on a solid foundation?

NOTES:

"God's Masterpiece"
Ephesians 2:10

DAY 9: DADDY'S GIRL

He makes me to lie down in green pastures;
He leads me beside the still waters. He restores my soul.
Psalm 23:2–3 NKJV

One of my favorite inspirational stories is that of a traveling businessman. The businessman was late for his flight, but reached the boarding gate just before it closed. Sweating and out of breath, he scanned his boarding pass at the counter and quickly made his way to the plane.

Arriving at his seat, he greeted his companions, a middle-aged woman sitting at the window and a little girl sitting on the aisle seat. After stowing his bag above, he took his place between them.

After the flight took off, he began a conversation with the little girl. She appeared to be about the same age as his daughter and was busy with her coloring book. He asked her a few usual questions, such as her age (eight), her hobbies (cartoons and drawing), as well as her favorite animal (horses are pretty, but she just loves cats). He found it strange that such a young girl would be traveling alone, but he kept his thoughts to himself and decided to keep an eye on her to make sure she was okay.

About an hour into the flight, the plane suddenly began experiencing extreme turbulence. The pilot came over the intercom and told everyone to fasten their seatbelts and remain calm, as they had encountered rough weather.

Several times over the next half hour the plane made drastic dips and turns, shaking all the while. Some people began crying, and many, like the woman in the window seat, were praying intently.

The man was sweating and clenching his seat as tightly as he could and exclaimed, "Oh my God!" with each increasingly violent shake of the plane.

Meanwhile, the little girl was sitting quietly beside him in her seat. Her coloring book and crayons were put away neatly in the seat pocket in front of her, and her hands were calmly resting on her legs. Incredibly, she didn't seem worried all.

Then, just as suddenly as it had begun, the turbulence ended. The pilot came on a few minutes later to apologize for the bumpy ride and to announce that they would be landing soon. As the plane began its descent, the man said to the little girl, "You are just a little girl, but I have never met a braver person in all my life! Tell me, dear, how is it that you remained so calm while all of us adults were so afraid?"

Looking at him in the eyes, she said, **"My father is the pilot, and he's taking me home."**

David found himself in some turbulence. In fact, in 2 Samuel 15, David found himself fleeing for his life as his own son, Absalom, and his forces hunted David down. It seemed to be one of the biggest storms of his life and may have been the time when he penned the words, "the Lord is my shepherd" (Psalm 23:1). In the midst of his turmoil, David assumed the role of a sheep and looked to his Shepherd for protection. Like the little girl on the plane, He knew His Father was the Shepherd and would take him home.

We live in a world of turbulent times, where many are overwhelmed with fear and anxiety. Fear for their future, health, children, finances, family, jobs, and even of people. It can be easy to jump into fear, worry, and panic, but why not be the one to ride out the story to see how it ends? Isn't that much more powerful? As we reflect on the storms and pressures of our lives, can we be identified as someone **who acts** like God is our Shepherd? How does God want us to respond to the anxiety in our lives? I would venture to say, like a "Daddy's girl."

A plethora of ways exist that one can be recognized as a Daddy's girl. One of the ways is the fact that she takes His word as gold. Psalm 23 gives us clear instructions from a Father that help us to respond to life's anxieties.

Lie Down

In the chaos of our lives, schedules, demanding jobs, and pressures of life, it is hard to slow down and "lie down." The first thing that the shepherd does with the sheep in the morning is to make them lie down in green pastures and feeds them until they are satisfied. Sheep can graze peacefully for hours, but they become anxious when food is scarce.

Spiritual hunger occurs when the word of God is lacking. So many people are suffering from hurry sickness and running on empty, burned out, and stressed out. A good shepherd knows where the water holes are and will lead his sheep to those places. Isaiah 26:3 says, "You will keep him in perfect peace, whose mind is stayed on You, because he trusts in You."

Take Care of Yourself

As you commit to thriving in true identity, make sure your soul isn't sick and stop doing things that cause sickness in the first place. Stop living by your feelings; stop holding onto unforgiveness. Stop living with regret and guilt from the past. Stop carrying everyone and neglecting yourself. Stop worrying and wasting today's strength fighting tomorrow's battles. Stop worrying about what God is already working on.

Your faith grows in unfamiliar places.

Grow Before You Go

In the children's game, "Red Light, Green Light," one of the rules is to not run too fast, or when "Red Light!" is called out, you will not be able to stop. If you are still moving when God calls "Red Light!" you may have to go back to the starting line.

Let God restore your soul, He will lead you in the right pathways as you move from striving to thriving in true identity.

We know how the story ends. "Surely goodness and mercy shall follow me all the days of my life; and I will dwell in the house of the Lord forever" (Psalm 23:6).

So remember, Daddy's girl, your Father is the Pilot, and He's taking you home.

1. What are the places in your life where you need to lie down?

2. What are the places in your life where you need to take better care of yourself?

3. Where can you pause and grow before you go?

DAY 10: WHEN LIFE CHANGES YOUR NAME

But she said to them, "Do not call me Naomi; call me Mara,
for the Almighty has dealt very bitterly with me.
Ruth 1:20 (NKJV)

Welcome Home! That was the sign I was holding when my daughter, Bianca, who was thoroughly enjoying a year-long cultural immersion Rotary Exchange, returned from Mexico because of the SARS pandemic. The look on her face when she walked off that plane burst the balloon of excitement I felt at seeing her after so long. She was having the best year of her life, only to have it aborted by a pandemic. Ten years later, my youngest, Courtney, who had started a job in the fashion industry in the UK, has returned home with the same look because of the COVID-19 pandemic.

Change can blindside us all. The one thing we know about change is that it is constant—especially now, *everything* is changing all around us. Whether we like it or not, change is the new norm and things are changing at a rapid pace.

In the book of Ruth, Naomi went through multiple major changes like a small boat at sea stuck in a storm: up and down, good and bad, hope and despair. She moved from Bethlehem to Moab with her husband, only to become a widow and lose her two sons to death, which left her destitute in the middle of a famine in the land. Her only hope was to return to Bethlehem where there was enough to eat. She left full and returned empty. Upon her return, she changed her name from Naomi (pleasant) to Mara (bitter).

Could it be that the sound of her name, Naomi, meaning "pleasant, lovely, delightful," only served to remind her of a life she once knew?

A name or reputation can shape a major part of your identity. What happens when that piece of your identity is threatened?

You may have been in a stable place and had the very foundation of your security shaken apart. Perhaps you were the big chief on your job, the head of your team, in a big home, top of your class, prom queen, student of the month, highest paid in your family, businessperson of the year, perfect couple…. But then came a major sea change or a "famine in the land," and now you find yourself in a dead-end job, failing in school, stagnant, divorced, in a bad relationship, in debt, unfulfilled, and you face a temptation to change your name. How do we ride the waves in a sea of change when life changes your name?

Trust God's Providence

Romans 8:28 says, "And we know that all things work together for good to those who love God, to those who are the called according to His purpose."

The book of Ruth is a story of the plan of God at work for His purpose. Naomi and Ruth were carried through difficult times by God's providential care, and He provided sustenance in the days of poverty. Naomi lost her sons, but God gave her Ruth, and ultimately, their path led them to be part of the lineage of Jesus Himself.

It's important to have spiritual eyesight and gain insight into the place where the providence of God sends you. If we magnify every difficulty, we get stuck and never go through with the work God has given us to do to get to His purpose for us.

Trust God's Plan

Trust God with the secret desires of your soul. You can be honest with God. When you allow life to change your name, there is an instant effect. You give up on your dreams and resort to a mindset of, "this is the hand I've been dealt." Naomi had the same mindset but had she stayed in that mentality, she and Ruth never would have met the purpose God had for them.

Have you given up on your dream? Let me encourage you, God has a vision for each one of us that we don't have the power to unsubscribe from. Jeremiah 29:11 says, "For I know the thoughts that I think toward you, says the Lord, thoughts of peace and not of evil, to give you a future and a hope."

Do you think you can halt God's plan for you? Oh, my sister, you are sadly mistaken. You *are* powHerful, but He is *all powerful*. No matter how much negative self-talk you engage in, or how many times life tries to rename you, you won't be able to change His mind about you or your future purpose. Remember the promise in Ephesians 3:20, "Now to Him who is able to do exceedingly abundantly above all that we ask or think, according to the power that works in us."

Look into God's heart and you will see your dream. It's time to wake up from your sleep and dream again! Let God defibrillate and reactivate your dream—let him shock you into mental shape and revive that dormant dream inside of you.

Don't allow temporary circumstances to discourage you. Be careful to not focus on the momentary failure so you miss the moment—each moment, even the hardships are preparing you for a lifetime. Don't let Satan make you become so focused on the failure that you lose the fight, so sick and tired that you lose your light, or so angry that you lose your salt. Failure isn't easy but rather than focusing on it, let it make you uncomfortable enough to spur you to action and change. It's an opportunity to embrace change so you can fly, soar, and thrive in your true identity!

Isaiah 43:1 says, "But now, thus says the Lord, who created you, O Jacob, and He who formed you, O Israel: 'Fear not, for I have redeemed you; I have called you by your name; you are Mine.'"

With so many changes happening in the world today, many are teetering on the precipice of a name change. Faced with massive changes, job loss, and family struggles, many are asking, "What do I do now?"

I think a great response is, as Winston Churchill once said, "Success is not final; failure is not fatal: it is the courage to continue that counts."

"God's Masterpiece"
Ephesians 2:10

1. What dream have you given up on?

_____

_____

_____

_____

_____

_____

_____

2. Where do you need the courage to continue? How can you get back up and continue on?

_____

_____

_____

_____

_____

_____

_____

_____

_____

NOTES:

DAY 11: WHEN JESUS CHANGES YOUR NAME

One of the two who heard John speak, and followed Him, was Andrew, Simon Peter's brother. He first found his own brother Simon, and said to him, "We have found the Messiah" (which is translated, the Christ). And he brought him to Jesus. Now when Jesus looked at him, He said, "You are Simon the son of Jonah. You shall be called Cephas."
John 1:40–42[2]

There was a moment last year while driving through the city, my car made one loud screeching sound, stalled for a second, and then stopped completely. It refused to go any further. I couldn't understand the problem because I had *just* had it serviced and everything was okay. I had it towed to the auto service shop, expecting a call at the end of the day letting me know my engine died, or that my car needed an expensive repair. Instead, the mechanic said the service was free. He said there was nothing wrong with the car; he just had to take it to an open field and run it! You see, I live on an island where we are only allowed to drive up to twenty miles per hour. My car, however, is "built for the road"—it is meant to go fast. My car generally drove well, but it wasn't allowed to live up to its full potential.

My experience reminded me of Simon, the fisherman. He was doing a good job as a fisherman, but he had not yet reached his full potential. Jesus came along, saw Simon's true purpose, and rerouted him. Jesus had to, for lack of a better word, "fire" Simon from his job as a fisherman. He was good at it, but he wasn't built for it. He was meant for more!

God doesn't dumb down His message. Sometimes God shuts a door because He knows what is in you, but you won't move out of a place of comfort. Simon was good at what he did, and sometimes being good at something can be a dangerous place because it can make you *comfortable*. God saw where Simon was and said, "You are" and, "You will be." *That* is how God sees us—in the fullness of what is possible and what we are capable of.

---

[2] The New King James translates Cephas as *A Stone*. Other translations translate it as *Peter*.

Don't wait for the door to shut on you. If you are not operating in your strengths, you are just surviving. You are not *thriving*. As it always does, eventually, a change will come along and disrupt your world, but why wait? What's keeping YOU from disrupting you?

Here's a question to think about: When was the last time you experienced a personal disruption and **changed the course of your own direction?** Ten years, ten months, ten days?

As women, we face enough obstacles from both subconscious and conscious bias against us. Add other layers, like your minority or socio-economic status on top of that, and the obstacles can seem insurmountable. It can feel like we never have the luxury of "sitting on our laurels." But when we are thriving in our true identity and purpose, we rise to the challenge and push ourselves to be better, stronger, wiser. But it is important, however, to know our "why" and our "who" as we rise. Why are we doing what we are doing, and who are we doing it to please? The answer to those questions helps us keep ourselves accountable to our why and thriving in our true identity in Christ.

If you are comfortable right now, you are not being challenged. And if you are not being challenged, you will not grow.

In ancient Greece and Israel, names *meant* something and told the people around you what you were all about. Jesus knew Simon's name and saw that he needed a change. He saw the potential for Simon ("reed"), the fisherman, to be Peter, the "rock" of the church. Within the boundaries of who he was, Simon wouldn't have been able to live up to his full potential, but when Jesus changed his name, the glass ceiling was shattered and Peter was able to be so much more.

In his letter to persecuted Christians in Asia Minor (1 Peter), Peter identifies himself as "Peter, an apostle of Christ." Even though he identifies himself and the identity of the author as the former fisherman is generally accepted throughout church history, some scholars have questioned if it might be someone else. They argue that the writing seems too advanced for a Galilean fisherman. However, look at what Peter says, "But you are a chosen race, a royal priesthood, a holy nation, a people for his own possession, that you may proclaim the excellencies of him who called you out of darkness into his marvelous light" (1 Peter 2:9). Peter remembered what Jesus did in changing him and left the church the same lesson, reaching farther into the future than his physical grasp could reach.

You and others may just see who you are, but God sees who you can become. You are not ordinary, not common, and not to be mistaken for the familiar.

Over the past decade, superheroes have gone from cult classics to mainstream popularity. Wonder Woman holds the undisputed position as the greatest superheroine of all time, and I especially loved the 2017 film. One quote that caught my attention and stuck out in my memory, was when millions were at risk of dying and Diana, princess of the Amazon, wanted to leave her people's secret refuge to help in the war. Her mother tells her, "If you choose to leave, you may never return." At that moment, Diana casts off the boundaries around her potential and steps into a new identity, becoming the superheroine we all know and appreciate so much for the inspiration she brings. She simply replies, "Who would I be if I stay?"

"God's Masterpiece"
Ephesians 2:10

1. What is a place of comfort where you might be stuck?

2. Who would you be if you stay in the place where you are?

DAY 12: FIRE THE FAMILIAR!

When He had come to His own country, He taught them in their synagogue, so that they were astonished and said, "Where did this Man get this wisdom and these mighty works? Is this not the carpenter's son? Is not His mother called Mary? And His brothers James, Joseph, Simon, and Judas? And His sisters, are they not all with us? Where then did this Man get all these things?"
Matthew 13:54–56

While I studied for my Ph.D., a fellow member of my cohort, Orlando, was one of my two study buddies. We studied, prayed, laughed, and encouraged each other through several challenging years, while we all juggled school with full-time jobs and families. Despite a long, arduous journey and as the last ones in the cohort to finish the course, we finished our race. On graduation morning, we agreed to celebrate with breakfast. I was always the last one to arrive—my classmates were used to that—but this time, my tardiness left us with no real time to fellowship and I felt horrible for cutting our time together short. Later, I received news that Orlando had been killed by a drunk driver on the highway. That short breakfast was our last fellowship together.

Our mutual friend, Jennie, and I watched his funeral online and were stunned by the outpouring of tributes and scholarship donations from all over the world. Orlando was involved in philanthropic work, giving, preaching, teaching, and building on nearly every continent, and had impacted hundreds of thousands of lives. Jen and I thought he was just our study buddy and friend, bonding as we struggled to pass statistics. We were too close to see his potential, too familiar with him to focus on his true identity.

The definition of the word *familiar* is, "well-known from long or close association." In Matthew 13, Jesus was snubbed by His own people as a result of their over-familiarity. They saw Jesus grow up and could only see Him as an ordinary person. They were so familiar with His family, his background, and His culture that they thought they knew Him. They put boundaries on His potential. Oftentimes, when we are too familiar with someone, we can take for granted the gifts they possess, until someone new comes along, and sees different treasures with fresh eyes and celebrates them.

The moral of one of Aesop's fables, *The Fox & the Lion* is, "familiarity breeds contempt." The implication is that if you know someone too long, you begin to dislike that person *because* you know too much about them. While that may be the case for some, I posit that the more concerning phenomenon is "familiarity breeds *contentment*."

In my former career in human resources, I watched so many managers lose talented team members because they became so familiar with their team that they took people for granted until another company came along and enticed them away. The managers would then scramble to try to keep their team together, but often, their efforts proved fruitless since the team members already felt underappreciated.

Yesterday, our focus was on areas in which we were too comfortable and how to disrupt ourselves so we could move *toward* a new place. Today, we're looking at what it looks like, practically, to move away *from* the familiar, in order to get to that new place. The hurdle you have to cross is familiarity—the enemy of your destiny.

Often, because of familiarity, people have preconceived notions about others, and those notions lead to doubt. Like Jesus, they end up rejected, cast aside. Even though Jesus grew up in Nazareth, His relatives and neighbors didn't know Him at all—not His true identity. They saw Him as the carpenter's son and nothing more. They could not see His potential.

Early in my Christian walk, one of my spiritual mentors told me not to cast my pearls to the swine (Matthew 7:6). Do not waste good things on people who will not appreciate them—they will only trample on them and crush them. Good things like your gifts, your dreams, and the vision for your life. Be careful not to share your dreams with dream killers. Dream killers are not always those who naysay at a distance. Sometimes, the dream killers are closer to you, those who think they know you so well and presuppose that you could never start that business, get that promotion, attend that school, or start that ministry. God wants you to know your true identity in Him so you don't fall into the trap of performing down to the level that others—even those close to you and who you feel a certain loyalty toward—expect of you, a phenomenon known as the Pygmalion Effect.

Many confuse loyalty with familiarity. A misplaced sense of loyalty might keep us in a place we are no longer meant to be. It's important to know the reason *why* you find yourself staying in familiar places or with familiar people. Sometimes, the best gift we can give ourselves is to fire the familiar.

Perhaps it is time. Do you have the courage to fire that familiar relationship that isn't growing, or the dream killers in the familiar friend group that doesn't build you up, but breaks you down? Sometimes people can be disguised as "good friends," but they are really ungodly soul ties based on emotional co-dependencies that use up all of your energy. When helping them begins to hurt you, it's time to fire that relationship.

Are you asking for spiritual direction from people who are familiar, but have never been where you want to go? We can sometimes tend to go to other women with our problems—that *is* what our sisters are for—but it's time to understand the difference between a familiar friend and a spiritual *mid-wife*. A familiar friend is someone who will sympathize with you and satisfy your current walk. A mid-wife is someone who will speak life into your future, challenge you, tell you the truth even when it's hard, and see the gold in you and push you until *you* see it too. A true mid-wife friend is someone who can make your dreams leap within you as John leaped in Elizabeth's womb when Mary entered the room (Luke 1:41).

While other people can become too familiar with us, many of us are guilty of becoming too familiar with God and taking Him for granted. We put Him in boxes, expecting specific things out of Him and stifling the potential of what He can do and how He can move in our lives. With any relationship, when we know the person will be there, we can lose our intentionality until a crisis comes along and snatches our attention and intention back to the relationship again.

Jesus is a friend (John 15:3) who sees the very best in you. He desires to fire you up so you can thrive in your true identity! But first, it's time to attend to the crisis at hand and fire the familiar!

1. What's the familiar in your life that you need to fire so you can thrive in true identity?

2. Remember Wonder Woman from yesterday? Who will *you* be if you stay in that familiar place?

3. Have you become too familiar with God? Do you still believe in the power of prayer? Or are you still praying the same simple, rote prayers you've always prayed?

"God's Masterpiece"
Ephesians 2:10

Then Elisha died, and they buried him. And the raiding bands from Moab invaded the
land in the spring of the year. So it was, as they were burying a man, that suddenly
they spied a band of raiders; and they put the man in the tomb of Elisha; and when the
man was let down and touched the bones of Elisha, he revived and stood on his feet.

2 Kings 13:20–21 NKJV

After a particularly hard year in high school, my daughter received a "Most Improved" award at an awards ceremony. She was shocked to even be invited, and entered the ceremony a slight hesitation because these types of ceremonies were typically for the best in class. It was the prizegiving speech, however, that came as the true surprise.

Typically prizegiving speeches are delivered to those who may be considered to the best and the brightest. The guest speaker for the night, a champion cyclist, however, delivered his speech with a twist. His focus was on what it is like to be compared to the "best and the brightest" when you are not part of that group. He talked about what it was like to be in the shadow of someone deemed great.

He'd attended the same school as his sister, who was considered a scholar, but he was a few classes behind her. He despised the start of every year because his teachers expected him to live up to her reputation. One day, he decided he would create his own path and move out of the shadow of his sister. He found that path through cycling, something that was uniquely him without the limitations of what others expected of him. He eventually went on to compete in the Summer Olympics and became successful in many other areas of his professional career.

Toward the end of the night, after the keynote speech, I could hardly hold back the tears when my daughter won a second award. This one was a monetary award for being a key player in starting a Human Rights movement through Amnesty International at her school—a unique path she chose for herself. While she wasn't at the top of the class, she was at the top of *her* class, thriving in her true identity.

How easy it is to compare ourselves to those who have gone before us or those whose shoes we are expected to fill. Elisha had some big shoes to fill—he was the successor to the prophet, Elijah. He was called to ministry by Elijah, presented the word of God through prophecy, advised and anointed kings, helped the needy, and performed several miracles. He received a double portion of his anointing and performed twice as many miracles as Elijah. Yet, in many ways, his story is overshadowed by his predecessor, Elijah, who ascended to heaven in a chariot of fire.

Elisha lived long, probably more than eighty years old, and yet his ministry only consumed one-quarter of that time, followed by a long period of silence. At his end, though the Spirit of Elijah was upon him, he was not sent to heaven in a chariot; he simply left the world on the common road of death. Because Elisha's ministry was so impactful, he may have had the expectation to go out like Elijah; instead, God did something surprisingly *different*.

After he was dead and buried, "the raiding bands from Moab invaded the land…as they were burying a man, that suddenly they spied a band of raiders; and they put the man in the tomb of Elisha; and when the man was let down and touched the bones of Elisha, he revived and stood on his feet" (2 Kings 13:20–21).

Elisha died and was buried, but when they cast the man into his grave, on touching Elisha's bones, he came alive!

The bones of Elisha have a powl Ierful message for us today! Something dead can bring life.

God Is Not Predictable

Take the limitations off God. He does not do things the same way. Oftentimes, when it appears you are in the shadow of someone who appears successful, the temptation is to measure yourself by similar accomplishments, and that may mean taking similar paths. It can leave you feeling less than, or that you don't measure up, but we are God's masterpiece; a designer's original.

Even the hairs on your head are numbered (Matthew 10:30). He will not reduce your value to being a carbon copy of anyone else.

God Can Still Use You at Your Lowest Point

You may have reached your lowest point yet, but it's time to rise from the graveyard of your mind. Even after his death, Elisha's impact was still powerful, even though he may have passed the traditional point of usefulness. Elisha died after forty-three years of not seeing a miracle, but God was not finished with him. There was still another miracle from the heap of bones in the grave—He used the dead bones to bring healing! Even in the midst of your darkest days, never forget that God is omnipotent—all-powerful. Life *can* come out of a heap of bones. The situation may be dead, but God is not. He is alive and because He lives, you can be restored.

Pick Up Your Dead Dreams

Perhaps all that remains of your dreams is a heap of bones (old notebooks, journals, or vision boards), but those bones are calling out. A miracle is still possible because the God of Israel is still alive. Let the God of your dreams revive them again!

Some of us have given up on our dreams because we think they are dead, or there has been a long period of silence. We stopped asking God for the big things, extraordinary things. Because we saw the enemy coming toward us, we dropped our dreams and our hopes in the grave. We stopped believing that God can do the impossible.

Today, God is allowing those hopes and dreams to be reactivated. Take up your bed and walk. There isn't time for a pity party. We serve a God who can do the big things. Why take a car with a powerful turbo engine and drive it twenty miles per hour? You have to run that thing to its maximum power. We serve a great big God, yet we play it safe and ask Him for the little things. Why not ask God for the big things? The things you could not do unless God *Himself* did it, like reviving dead things.

God hears the dry bones of our dreams crying out and wants to revive our hearts so we can rise up from our graves, live again, and thrive in our true identities! What are you excited about? If your answer is nothing, you need revival! Both the bones of the Apostles and of Elisha are shouting out today. The bones of a loved one of many years ago, maybe a mother, who spent many hours on her knees praying that her children would thrive in their true identity! Those bones are calling for a decision. Put your trust in Christ today, while you still have time, because on the day when your own body has finally been reduced to a heap of bones, it will be too late.

REFLECTIONS:

1. Whose shadow have you lived under?

2. What dreams need to be revived for you to thrive in your true identity?

NOTES:

DAY 14: OVERLOOKED

Jesus, knowing that the Father had given all things into His hands, and that He had come from God and was going to God, rose from supper and laid aside His garments, took a towel and girded Himself.

John 13:3–4 NKJV

Several years ago, I faced the prospect of a promotion. Someone left my company, and I had—in my view—done everything to prepare myself. A superior approached me about the role and I expressed interest. A few days later, they communicated that I would have the position and I didn't have to worry.

That same night, I was at a social gathering and someone outside the organization asked me where I worked. when I told him, he proceeded to tell me how excited he was that his friend had just received a job offer—for the role I had been promised. The next day I left for vacation, by God's grace. While gone, I received the call to formally advise me that someone else got the job and the leader would meet with me upon my return. Too late; I was already heartbroken. I was overlooked.

The same leader who promised me the position was mine came to my office when I returned. I will never forget his words that day, "I know I promised you the job and gave it to someone else, and I know I should say I am sorry, but the 'big boss' said if I do that, it is a sign of weakness, so I am not going to say sorry." Then he walked out without even waiting for my response.

That declaration was worse than not getting the job. Not only was I overlooked, I was disregarded. Sitting in disbelief for a moment, I watched him walk away from my office and down the hall and the only thing that came to mind was, "I choose to forgive."

I was surprised but not shaken, and I was not bitter. I know who I am, and I know Whose I am. My identity was not in that promotion. My identity was in Jesus Christ. I, therefore, knew that my work would continue as unto the Lord (Colossians 3:23–25). I will never forget what he said because that day, I learned to embrace the fullness of the text found in Philippians 4:12–13, "I know how to be abased, and I know how to abound. Everywhere and in all things I have learned both to be full and to be hungry, both to abound and to suffer need. I can do all things through Christ who strengthens me."

Whenever I am tempted to let bitterness enter my heart and begin to take root, I focus on Jesus when He washed His own disciple's feet. He knew who He was and He knew from whom He had come. More than that, He knew the power that was in His hands. Because Jesus knew His value in God, He could humble himself and serve. His identity came from God and not from His earthly position.

If you have been overlooked, invisible, underappreciated, or disregarded, it is time to look up and take a heavenly perspective. God sees you and He knows who you are. He gives you your identity and all promotion comes from Him.

Several women written about in the Bible were overlooked. Shiphrah and Puah were two of those women. They barely made it in the Old Testament, but they play a vital role in the population of Israel. As Hebrew midwives, they briefly prevented a genocide of children by the Egyptians, according to Exodus 1:15–21. God blessed Shiphrah and Puah by giving them families of their own, and later, Moses was born. These women might have been easily overlooked, but they left a lasting legacy.

Perhaps you've been overlooked. Rejection is just another form of direction. God sees you, and His plan for you remains. Or perhaps you feel like you grew up as an invisible child. That kind of childhood wound has long-term implications that can cause you to be challenged as an adult. You might constantly feel the need to fight for your value, trying everything to prove your worth. When no one is there to appreciate your value, it leaves a void where your identity belongs; it leaves a hole in your heart.

When you feel overlooked, don't look down. Satan can make you feel defeated, unworthy, or unqualified, but you don't have to stay there. Look up! The book of Hebrews says, "Looking unto Jesus, the author and finisher of our faith, who for the joy that was set before Him endured the cross, despising the shame, and has sat down at the right hand of the throne of God." (Hebrews 12:2–3)

Whenever you start to feel put down, all you have to do is *look up*.

"God's Masterpiece"
Ephesians 2:10

1. When have you been overlooked?

2. What can you do to keep looking up?

NOTES:

Glowing Up

DAY 15: FRESH START

Then the dove came to him in the evening, and behold, a freshly plucked olive leaf was in her mouth; and Noah knew that the waters had receded from the earth. So he waited yet another seven days and sent out the dove, which did not return again to him anymore.

Genesis 8:11–12

As we begin the first day of the Glowing Up section of our study, I am reminded of the olive branch. Who would have thought that something so small could have such significance?

Some of you may recall Nelson Mandela extending the olive branch. The action means to make an offer of peace or reconciliation. While it is commonly used in political settings, the term has Biblical origins in the story of Noah. Before the olive branch can be extended, however, there is a process.

In the story of Noah's ark, when the waters began to slowly recede, Noah sent two birds out of the ark, first a raven and later a dove. He sent the dove a second time, and it returned that evening with an olive branch in its mouth. An olive tree, while it can grow in mountainous areas, typically reaches full height at fifty feet tall. With the olive branch, Noah knew that low trees were now visible over the floodwaters and that they hadn't been destroyed by the flood—the most vital piece of data.

With that find, Noah now knew some critical things that would help him assess how to have a fresh start. We can take a page out of the life and cycle of the low branches of the olive tree.

Sometimes, we can find ourselves in low places, whether we've experienced a loss, negative self-talk, comparison, the judgment of others, past guilt, death, divorce—any dark thing can shove us off the path God has for us and into a place of waiting—a low place.

Just because you find yourself in a low place doesn't mean you have to stay low. You may feel invisible, in the background, in a quiet season of your life, where, on the surface, it looks like nothing is happening, but remember the olive branch? You may have been underwater, but you didn't drown (Isaiah 43:2).

Some time ago, while running through London's Gatwick Airport, I came across a sign that reminded me of the real significance of being in a low place. The sign read, "Powering Up in the Charging Zone." In order to experience a fresh start, we must first allow ourselves to experience the *charging zone*.

The Charging Zone

This is the invisible or forgotten place, the place where we "powHer" up and wait with expectation! We are not like those who wait with no hope. When we no longer expect the outpouring of the Spirit, it can feel like we get no response from God, or like the saying goes, "the heavens become as brass." Because we see no cloud above our heads, we expect no rain, but strength comes in the waiting.

The kind of strength that's built in the waiting *cannot* be built anywhere else! It sets you up for the next phase of the journey—because you cannot go on without it. The weight of the wait is where He strengthens our spiritual muscles.

In this place, we learn to build resilience, engaging in crawling exercises like prayer and faith to strengthen your spiritual core. When you were a new Christian, you could barely lift a twenty-pound weight of a problem, but as you learned to wait on God, you began to lift that hundred-pound weight and hold! Your capacity ought to have changed. There is a famous quote by Muhammad Ali who said that "The man who views the world at fifty the same as he did at twenty has wasted thirty years of his life." [3]There should have been some growth.

---

[3] Source, Business Insider

Waiting will shift your perspective and help you to see things differently. When you look back over your life, aren't you glad you waited and didn't make haste? Psalm 27:14 says, "Wait on the Lord; be of good courage, and He shall strengthen your heart; wait, I say, on the Lord!" Whatever plans He has for you in the end, I promise, they will be worth the wait!

When you're in a low place, it takes time to rise, soar, and flourish again. When it's time, you have to move from the charging zone to the No Wake Zone.

The No-Wake Zone

In nautical terms, entering a "no-wake zone" means boats must reduce to the slowest speed they can travel while still maintaining the ability to steer and make forward progress. When vessels move at these speeds, they produce a minimum wake—the disturbance of the water behind the boat. When people in the church have been bruised, they need time to heal before they can be put back in the pulpit or sent out in ministry, or else they run the risk of making waves and causing (often unintentional) disturbances in other people's lives.

With the deliverance of the olive branch, Noah knew that treetops were visible, but he also understood something else. If the dove returned to him so quickly—or at all—it meant that the dove could not find a proper place to nest. Why couldn't the dove nest on that olive tree? Simply put, birds build nests of twigs on the ground. The nature of the dove in particular is that it will only put its foot down in something peaceful.

Of the hundreds of possible tree leaves to reappear after the earth was covered with water, the dove found the leaf of a tree created by God to produce olives. When crushed, the olives from the olive trees produce olive oil. The olive leaf in the mouth of the dove speaks to us that out of the crises and storms of life, the Holy Spirit will bring us an olive branch and help us to slowly make our way back to His path, making peace with ourselves and with others along the way.

This slow reconciliation allows us to power up in the "no wake zone." It allows us to heal and come to a place of power in that healing. The dove came back the first time because it wasn't the right time for Noah and company to exit the arc—the earth still had more healing to do, it needed to be empowered to hold humanity again. Sometimes, energized by the promise and eager for the fulfillment, we try to step out into God's plans for us too soon, but our hearts aren't right yet, it's too soon in the process. We must first go through a rediscovery of self, a realignment of values, a re-establishing of boundaries, and a rebuilding of relationships. Only once that process is complete can we be ready to move forward into the Fueling Zone.

The Fueling Zone

The fueling zone is a place to be filled and fueled to be able to pour out. It is the Power Share Zone where you are powered up, but for a purpose— to reproduce.

I recall Samsung announcing its new Galaxy S10, a phone that can wirelessly charge *other* phones. While this idea was novel to consumers, this concept is nothing new to the kingdom of God. God gives us *dunamis* power—inherent power capable of reproducing itself like a dynamo. In the fueling zone, we are "powHered up" to "powHer share."

We are like olive trees (Psalm 1). The olive tree develops slowly, but often attains a ripe old age of *several centuries*. If cut down, new shoots spring up from its roots, so that as many as five new trunks could come into being. Its root system is very robust and capable of regenerating the tree even if the above-ground structure is destroyed. The older an olive tree is, the broader and more gnarled its trunk appears.

Even when we are crushed by life's struggles, our fruit remains. We are crushed only to pour out, like oil. We fall so we can lift others up. Our branches have power—when we rise and extend, our branches help to bring healing and new hope to our sisters around us. We are "daughters of oil."

We go through a process during fresh starts because, in that new season, God wants us to be filled and fueled with His power. We are powHered up to powHer share! *Now* you are ready for a fresh start!

Let us strive to burn with the zeal of God, and to produce good fruit, filled with the oil of God's Holy Spirit.

I'm reminded that in the book of Job, we read, "Though your beginning was insignificant, yet your end will increase greatly" (Job 8:7 NASB). If you're looking for a fresh start, no matter what zone you're in or what your backstory looks like, a new beginning is always possible.

"God's Masterpiece"
Ephesians 2:10

1. What zone are you in right now?

2. Are you ready for a fresh start?

DAY 16: BLOOM

Blessed is the man who trusts in the Lord, and whose hope is the Lord. For he shall be like a tree planted by the waters, which spreads out its roots by the river, and will not fear when heat comes; but its leaf will be green, and will not be anxious in the year of drought, nor will cease from yielding fruit.

Jeremiah 17:7–8

I am a self-confessed introvert. That seems odd to some because all my work involves relating to people one-on-one and in large groups. My number one strength from the Strength Finder index, however, is "Relator," and I love working with people. Being an introvert just means I recharge in quiet, alone time. The strongly introverted side of me plays out when someone wants to host a celebration for me. Hence the reason, I strategically planned my last day with my previous employer prior to starting my business.

I purposefully made my last day on April thirteenth, when I would be teaching in the United States. I did not even tell my U.S. team that it was my last day on the job. I also did not tell the conference center, where I had been a frequent speaking guest for the prior ten years, that it was my last visit. My plan was to send everyone a lovely letter after I was gone.

That was not to be. Somehow, the word got out. My U.S. team held a dinner for me. The conference center gathered all their staff and surprised me with a personalized basket and a card that everyone signed—from the general manager to every maid who ever serviced my usual room, #204. They had no idea that every time I visited (which was every month for several years), it was a personal struggle. But I was where God had placed me for that season. Finally, when I returned home, my team had me return to the office so they could host a company-wide party for me. Needless to say, I was overwhelmed, but I was a good sport and held it together until, during the party, they showed a video with clips of people from all the different departments sharing what I meant to them. At that point, I broke down and cried. I just had no idea that my presence could make that much of a difference.

That night, the phrase that rang in my ears was, "bloom where you are planted." It is a popular phrase that many believe is in Scripture, but it actually isn't a scriptural text. Rather, the *sentiment* can be found in Scripture. The popular phrase means "to be fruitful," to make the best of life wherever you are in your present circumstances. Many attribute the phrase to an American graphic artist and illustrator named Mary Englebreit in her book, *The Art and the Artist*.

While Englebreit made the phrase popular, Saint Francis de Sales (1567–1622), originally coined the phrase when he was the bishop of Geneva. He is recorded saying, "Truly charity has no limit; for the love of God has been poured into our hearts by His Spirit dwelling in each one of us, calling us to a life of devotion and inviting us to bloom in the garden where He has planted and directing us to radiate the beauty and spread the fragrance of His Providence."

Lydia was one woman in the book of Acts who bloomed where she was planted (Acts 16:11–15). She was a businesswoman, known for selling purple goods. While they were beautiful, her beauty radiated most from the hospitality she showed to others. She glowed up and the transformation of her life was evidenced by her eagerness to show missionaries hospitality in her home. Lydia's house was the place where the Christians gathered to receive Paul's final encouragement before he left the area—all because of her spiritual glow.

Guard your spiritual glow with God's grace, as Lydia did, even while she took care of her business affairs and other pursuits, which were not to be compared with her kingdom purpose. Sadly, we are all guilty of allowing our secular jobs or the stresses of life to rob us of our glow. Instead of focusing on things above, we become distracted and frustrated with things below. You are planted where you are during this season for a reason. There could be just one person who needs you there and they are looking for your light.

Jesus told us there would be people who would need to see our light and left words to encourage us. "You are the salt of the earth; but if the salt loses its flavor, how shall it be seasoned? It is then good for nothing but to be thrown out and trampled underfoot by men. You are the light of the world. A city that is set on a hill cannot be hidden. Nor do they light a lamp and put it under a basket, but on a lampstand, and it gives light to all who are in the house. Let your light so shine before men, that they may see your good works and glorify your Father in heaven" (Matthew 5:13–16).

I love the lyrics to the song, *Brighten the Corner Where You Are*:

> *Do not wait until some deed of greatness you may do,*
> *Do not wait to shed your light afar,*
> *To the many duties ever near you now be true,*
> *Brighten the corner where you are.*

Satan will try hard to blow your candle out with all kinds of tactics to wear you down and make you lose your true identity, and even worse, pick up the fragments of someone else's identity. That is because he knows, the light you shine will draw someone else closer to Christ.

Instead, shine brightly and bloom where you are planted!

1. What has robbed you of your glow?

2. Who may be impacted if you don't allow your light to shine?

3. What spiritual controls can you put in place to guard your glow?

Therefore, if anyone is in Christ, he is a new creation; old things have passed away; behold, all things have become new.
2 Corinthians 5:17

There seems to be a trend that when Presidents of the United States are elected for a second term, the first ladies become more confident in having a voice and finding a meaningful cause to support as an advocate. Michelle Obama, the first lady of the forty-fourth President of the United States is one recent example. She advocated for many causes such as "Let's Move" to address the challenge of childhood obesity, "Joining Forces" to ensure that service members, veterans, and their families have the tools they need to succeed throughout their lives, "Reach Higher" to inspire young people across America to take charge of their future by completing their education past high school, and "Let Girls Learn," which calls on countries across the globe to help educate and empower young women.

One of her advocacy passions, however, is one many don't speak as much about and that is the integral role she has played in being a voice for helping to preserve the monarch butterfly, which has been suffering from a severely declining population. On June 20, 2014, President Barack Obama issued a presidential memorandum entitled, "Creating a Federal Strategy to Promote the Health of Honeybees and Other Pollinators."

What I find interesting is that her advocacy for the butterfly very much seems to parallel her own life. At one stage of her life, one might suggest that Michelle was in the cocoon of a regular working-class Chicago neighborhood of humble beginnings, to undergoing a metamorphosis from the cocoon to a caterpillar, as she gave birth to her career to fully spreading her butterfly wings in the White House. Her book *Becoming* was indicative of someone who has transformed into a "butterfly" and could no longer be expected to dwell in the "cocoon." It also relays a message to us that what we see today didn't happen overnight. It took time and it took some growing pains.

Transformation happens through process of changing completely. The key word is *process*. Transformation doesn't take place in an instant. The butterfly must go through all stages of its growth. If the process is disrupted, the butterfly will either die or its wings will not develop, rendering it unable to fly.

We too must experience the stages of spiritual growth and development before we experience the "glow up" or metamorphosis, which is the end result of the change. We are primed, however, to want to reach the "glow up" before the "grow up." Romans 12:2 says, "And do not be conformed to this world, but be transformed by the renewing of your mind, that you may prove what is that good and acceptable and perfect will of God."

It all starts with the renewing of our minds. Our mindset matters. We cannot enter a new season with an old mindset. This is what happens when the mighty power of the Holy Spirit takes hold of us and transforms our lives. It involves learning and growing before glowing. It's the growing pains that people don't see that makes the glow up look so easy, but it is only after God has shaped us, molded us, and placed us on the Potter's wheel do we arise and start to thrive.

There can be no oil without the crushing of the olive. The change cycle involves letting go, being agile, and making a decision to embrace a new way of thinking. Putting pride, ego, and unforgiveness aside, and being willing to go through the purging process so that you can arise, spread your wings, and fly. It is impossible to fly with the burden of heaviness deeply rooted in those things that put us back in the cocoon. The butterfly never goes back to its caterpillar state.

Jesus had come to the place of no longer being under His parents' wings as He once knew, to spreading His butterfly wings and going about the work of the kingdom. When His parents were looking for Him, His response was, "Why did you seek Me? Did you not know that I must be about My Father's business?" (John 2:49) His parents were looking for the Jesus they'd always known, but Jesus had experienced the glow up.

As you experience the beauty of emerging as a butterfly, you can find comfort in this text, "being confident of this very thing, that He who has begun a good work in you will complete it until the day of Jesus Christ" (Philippians 1:6).

1. What growing pains are you currently experiencing?

2. What are the areas tempting you to go back to your cocoon?

3. What do you need to keep spreading your wings?

DAY 18: BUTTERFLY EFFECT

So the Lord said to him, "What is that in your hand?"
He said, "A rod."
Exodus 4:2

When a butterfly flaps its wings in one part of the world, it can eventually cause a hurricane in another.

In 1963, Edward Lorenz presented this hypothesis to the New York Academy of Science and everyone laughed. This theory later became known in pop culture, as the Butterfly Effect. The concept is that small events can have large consequences.

Each one of us is like that butterfly, and each tiny move toward a positive mindset can make a positive difference in our homes, workplaces, churches, and communities. Similarly, small shifts in our thinking can lead to massively positive outcomes.

One conventional way of thinking that requires a shift is the approach to our own personal growth, which is to focus on fixing our own weaknesses. Remember attending your child's parent-teacher conferences and focusing on the one bad grade that he or she received? You may also recall receiving your last performance evaluation at work and rushing toward the lowest scores or weaknesses. Your mind might have immediately raced to what you can do to raise that score—or worse—if you can ever thrive in that area. This thought process can be soul destroying and the impact far reaching if you only focus on moving from an D grade to a C+. But what if you focused on at least one major strength and thought about a way to maximize it to its fullest potential?

The Lord used this strength-based approached and challenged Moses to shift his thinking in Exodus 4:2, when Moses focused on a plethora of weaknesses that would disqualify him from leading the people out of slavery. One might think his excuses were quite rational. After all, he spent his first many years in a strong position of favor and privilege, only to have one event change the course of his life, sending him running for forty years. He may have been justified to deem himself unqualified based on his reputation in the eyes of the Egyptians. But God knew who He was.

> Then Moses answered and said, "But suppose they will not believe me or listen to my voice; suppose they say, 'The Lord has not appeared to you.'"
> So the Lord said to him, "What is that in your hand?"
> He said, "A rod."

Moses continued, however, to say he was not eloquent enough in his speech, and further, how God should appoint someone else more qualified to do the job. The Lord asked Moses, "Who made your mouth?" (Exodus 4:11) and reminded him that He was aware of Aaron's strong communications skills that would be used to support the mission. The Lord, however, was intentional about making Moses focus on the one thing, his key strength, the thing that was in his hand. Moses took his one thing (his rod) and stretched out his hand with it to part the Red Sea.

Moses' one thing was his rod. Your one thing might be your talents, gifts, skills, finances, influence, or resources. One event can change the course of your direction. One word can change the way you see yourself. One failure can make you feel unqualified. One person's perception can make you doubt yourself. One small shift in thinking, can lead to massively positive outcomes. One tiny ripple can create far-reaching effects. One tiny action of yours can change many lives.

1. What is in your hand today?

2. In what ways have you tried to disqualify yourself?

3. What is one small shift in thinking you need to change to thrive in your true identity?

4. What small action will you say yes to today?

"God's Masterpiece"
Ephesians 2:10

It is not for you to know the times or periods that the Father has set by his own authority. But you will receive power when the Holy Spirit has come upon you; and you will be my witnesses in Jerusalem, in all Judea and Samaria, and to the ends of the earth.

Acts 1:7–8

One of the most effective forms of witness is often Christian leadership. As basketball fan, I enjoy watching a university competition in America called March Madness. In 2019, I watched the victory of the University of Virginia. Virginia coach Tony Bennett was outspoken about his Christian faith and acknowledged how it shapes his work with players. Bennett has cited his faith with helping to shape his coaching philosophy and the use of *Five Pillars*: humility, passion, unity, servanthood, and thankfulness. Those pillars can be seen through many of Bennett's players who he helps to *lift up* so they can *glow up*.

In this text from the book of Acts, Jesus gives his followers a vocation—witnessing—which is more than evangelizing. This vocation is about lifting others up.

We glow up by lifting up. Aquilla and Priscilla mentored Paul when he arrived in Corinth. He worked with this dynamic couple in their tentmaking business. While they may have already been Christians, they worked together in the shop and in evangelistic outreach, Priscilla and Aquila had the opportunity to be taught and trained personally by the apostle Paul.

Having been trained by Paul, Aquilla and Priscilla in turn worked with Apollos. He was very talented but had some gaps in his development. They privately mentored him with wisdom and tact. Every leader is called to shape other leaders. When you make this calling a priority, you identify gifts to be "stirred up" (2 Timothy 1:6). You pour into people through mentoring others, spending time, equipping classes, and taking people under your wings.

Barnabas was also a lifter of people. He knew how to add value to others. This contribution of empowerment can be seen through his interaction with Paul, which is a witness model we too can follow by:

1. Giving people a chance – Barnabas believed in Paul before anyone else did. He didn't wait until the apostles endorsed Paul before believing in him. He used the Holy Spirit to guide him in seeing the potential in Paul and encouraged him.

2, Recognizing the value of people around you – Barnabas endorsed Paul's leadership to other leaders. Barnabas took Paul and brought him to the disciples and told Paul's story. One of the best things leaders can do is to praise their people for a job well done.

3. Giving people a lift – Barnabas empowered Paul to reach his full potential. When Paul was assigned to help the church in Antioch, he found Paul and made him his companion. That one action empowered Paul to take his first assignment as a leader.

Whenever I invited guests to speak during my leadership classes, someone in the audience would always ask them what was pivotal in their career. Time and time again, they said, it was a sponsor, a mentor, a coach—someone who lifted them up.

In the words of Booker T. Washington, "If you want to lift yourself up, lift up someone else."

Where is your Jerusalem, Judea, and Samaria? Is it your job, your family, church school, and social clubs. Ultimately, the effect of the Holy Spirit is to take all God has given us— our gifts, experiences, passions, and knowledge —and set them to work, bringing glory to Christ in the church and in the world by lifting others up. We can then experience the ultimate **glow up!**

1. Who has helped to lift you up?

2. Where is your Jerusalem, Judea and Samaria?

3. Who can you help to lift up?

_____

_____

_____

_____

_____

_____

_____

_____

"God's Masterpiece"
Ephesians 2:10

DAY 20: UNCOVERED

Behold, You desire truth in the inward parts,
And in the hidden part You will make me to know wisdom.
Psalm 51:6

Throughout the past years, storytelling has become more widespread. Even amongst women there has been an emphasis on telling our stories. There's something about hearing another person's story that strengthens, empowers, and encourages the heart. People tend to see the end of the story, and if it's a successful ending, think it might not be attainable for them. But, they probably don't know from where you started and the trials you had to endure along the way. In fact, if they told you, you wouldn't believe them, and you would likely say, "Don't make me laugh." It would not be the kind of laughter people could hear on the other side of the room, but the silent laugh of disbelief.

There are many kinds of laughter. Besides the kind that makes us laugh in disbelief, there's the kind that brings us to tears. Then there are times when a situation catches us so off guard, we do not know whether to laugh or cry. We have experienced all these emotions at some time or another.

Sarah, the wife of Abraham, experienced different kinds of laughter in her lifetime, but not the everyday kind of laughing we normally think of. Sarah's laughter represented pivotal points in her life. One of those pivotal points was when all she wanted was a child of her own, but it appeared she'd never have one. She ran the risk of losing her identity and becoming a stigma in her community.

Although she had received the divine promise that from her womb that nations would spring, the possibility of ever becoming a mother died in her heart—until one day some visitors showed up at Abraham's tent and told him, "This time you know next year, Sarah will have a child." Sarah overheard and her reaction in Genesis 18:12–14 was as follows:

Therefore Sarah laughed within herself, saying, "After I have grown old, shall I have pleasure, my lord being old also?"

And the LORD said to Abraham, "Why did Sarah laugh, saying, 'Shall I surely bear a child, since I am old?' Is anything too hard for the LORD? At the appointed time I will return to you, according to the time of life, and Sarah shall have a son."

Sarah laughed because she no longer believed! Even when she heard the promise, she didn't believe it in her heart. She thought she was too old. She thought it was too late. A belief is defined as an acceptance of the mind that something is true. Sarah tried to deny her laughter, but God knows the hidden parts. The hidden thing that was in her heart was uncovered.

If we're honest with ourselves, we all have hidden things in our hearts that can lead to insecurities and the way we see ourselves. Then someone comes along and sees the hidden potential in us, and we sometimes secretly laugh. But God hears our laughter!

Despite Sarah's secret unbelief that God would fulfill His promise, not only did God give her the thing she most desired, He gave her so much more. Sarah was not just a mother to Isaac. She was a mother to a nation. She was an ancestor in the lineage of Jesus Christ.

We then, like Sarah, go to lengths to hide our secret laughter and act like we believe. We try desperately to cover it up. But God removes the veil of false beliefs and puts us in positions where He shows Himself strong on our behalf. Even when we don't think we can, He knows what we are made of and He knows who we are. He will show up and allow us to still **glow up!**

1. What promises from the word of God about your future have secretly made you laugh?

2. What do you need to do to believe again?

DAY 21: IMPOSTER SYNDROME

Casting down arguments and every high thing that exalts itself against the knowledge of God, bringing every thought into captivity to the obedience of Christ.
2 Corinthians 10:5

I started facilitating management courses in my early thirties. One day, as I opened my class by introducing myself, I was interrupted by one of the participants, an experienced manager, (who was approximately twenty years older than me). He boldly asked me in front of the whole class, "What qualifies you to teach the class?" He went on to ask, "what could you possibly offer the class given your age?"

As if that was not enough, he ended by saying he was very busy and preferred not to waste his time. I was stunned by the barrage of questions and embarrassed by the implied lack of competency. I then began to experience the dreadful fear that he might be right. *Was I an imposter? Was I pretending to be something that I was not?*

Through God's wisdom and grace, we had a successful session that day, but that was the first and certainly not last) time I experienced this phenomenon called the *Imposter Syndrome*, which nearly paralyzed me. The Imposter Syndrome is an overwhelming, persistent feeling of inadequacy, despite evident success; it is accompanied by the fear that one day you will be rejected or exposed. One of the signs of the Imposter Syndrome is a feeling of consistent self-doubt, such as fear of success, failure, or self-sabotage.

Imposter Syndrome is the silent dimmer of your glow. As you begin to glow up, you may encounter your own Imposter Syndrome moments in whatever environment or situation you find yourself. Satan will try to put up a smokescreen to make you feel that you do not belong where you are or do not have the ability to glow up to the next level. You may experience those Imposter Syndrome moments when starting a new job, taking on a new responsibility, getting married, becoming a first-time parent, entering a new educational program, or starting your own business.

He will use whatever tactics he can to ramp up your efforts to fulfill God's promise by yourself or prove your worth. He will fool you into thinking you have to work five times harder, keep getting more qualifications, go above and beyond, all to ensure you are not uncovered. While sometimes it may be necessary to engage in another level of commitment, the line is drawn when all your efforts are motivated by the desperate need to "not be found out" or uncovered.

Imposter Syndrome is a lie designed to paralyze you and keep you from moving forward. In Luke 5, Jesus reveals His identity to Peter by filling his nets with fish after Peter put in so much effort, toiling all night without success. After Peter experienced this breakthrough, one would think he would be excited. Instead, he fell to his knees, declaring how unworthy he was to have received such a miracle, based on his shortcomings. Jesus did not validate any of his fears. He only responded by saying: "Do not be afraid. From now on you will catch men." In other words, you are about to **glow up!**

Imposter Syndrome focuses inward. The real issue isn't so much that you feel bad about yourself. The real issue is that Imposter Syndrome paralyzes you; it's a stalling tactic that keeps you from moving forward. I believe it is one of the most significant areas that threatens your glow. As long as you are focused on your inability rather than God's ability, you will expand your efforts but shrink your prayers, goals, and ultimately your potential.

Isaiah 26:3 helps us to focus upward. "You will keep him in perfect peace, Whose mind is stayed on You, Because he trusts in You."

The more you try to prove your self-worth, the more you expose your self-doubts. Are you tired of putting in all your efforts to validate your identity? Matthew 11:28 gives us instruction:

Come to Me, all you who labor and are heavy laden, and I will give you rest. Take My yoke upon you and learn from Me, for I am gentle and lowly in heart, and you will find rest for your souls. For My yoke is easy and My burden is light.

*****

To be loved but not known is comforting but superficial. To be known and not loved is our greatest fear. But to be fully known and truly loved is, well, a lot like being loved by God. It is what we need more than anything. It liberates us from pretense, humbles us out of our self-righteousness, and fortifies us for any difficulty life can throw at us.
– Timothy Keller

Rest in the fact that Jesus already paid the price on the cross, so you can always have the assurance that you belong. You belong in that role, in that calling—wherever He has placed you, you belong!

1. Are you experiencing the Imposter Syndrome in any area of your life?

2. Do you feel as though you haven't earned your position, title, or standing in the family, (despite numerous degrees, generosity, and achievements), so you feel pressed to do more than those around you to prove your worth?

3. What will you do to find peace and move forward?

_____

_____

_____

_____

_____

_____

_____

_____

PART

4

Showing Up

DAY 22: AS YOURSELF

And the second, like it, is this: "You shall love your neighbor as yourself."
There is no other commandment greater than these.
Mark 12:31

I used to be rather good in a game called Netball, up until the age of nine years old. At the age of ten, however, I had quite a serious accident, injuring my eye, and could no longer see the ball with the same degree of accuracy. Because of that circumstance, someone decided I was not allowed to go to physical education classes for the remainder of my elementary school years. Eventually, as I moved on to high school, I could attend PE class, but was considered to have butterfly fingers—fingers that cannot catch the ball. Therefore, I was also the very last person to be selected on every team, every time.

The whole experience of being a bystander from my early years and being rejected all through high school gave me a complex about any form of physical exercise. I had gotten by with sporadic spurts of walking regimes, but had never been serious about establishing an exercise routine.

That is until a doctor's report showed that my numbers had shifted and given me reason for concern. I immediately took action, engaged a personal trainer, and have been consistent in my efforts for the past few years.

To date, I cannot recall one single session I did not dread. In fact, I always go kicking and screaming and have to engage in self-talk every time—hence the reason I cannot trust myself yet to join voluntary classes. Despite my complaining, admittedly, I have never felt better. I have learned one thing through experience—the importance of **showing up**.

The most important place to show up is for yourself. As women, we are often primed to show up for everyone else. We are naturally nurturers. We will make sure everyone else is taken care of, but when it comes to showing up for ourselves, many of us have been guilty of putting ourselves last. This can lead us to a place of pouring out from an empty vessel. Remember the Shepherd in our earlier devotion, who leads his sheep beside the still waters? If he doesn't lead, then the sheep will continue to walk around and around the water pots but never stop and drink. Psalm 23 give us some basic principles to live by that bring balance to the mind, body, and soul.

Basic principles or rules to live by help us to navigate life and give us direction. For years, we have been taught to live by the golden rule: "Do unto others as you would have them do unto you." Later, author Stephen Covey introduced the Platinum Rule: "Do unto others as they would have you do unto them." Mark 12:31, however, tells us to "love your neighbor as yourself."

Loving your neighbor as yourself is so important to God that not only is it a command, but it appears eight times in the Bible. Before you can go on this journey, you must receive God's love and know you are deeply loved (1 John 4:10). You cannot give what you do not have. You have to receive love before you can pour it out.

What does it mean to love our neighbor? When we show up for those around us and truly exhibit love, we forgive them, grant them the grace they need, show compassion, look out for their wellbeing, speak kindly to them, encourage them with the Word during tough times or failures, and naturally pray for them. Now that is a good checklist. Review that checklist and ask yourself, are you loving yourself that way? If you are to love our neighbor as yourself, **how are you loving yourself?**

What does the portrait of *loving yourself* look like? What would the caption under your masterpiece say? Would you feel confident and comfortable sharing it with a neighbor whom you wanted to show the full extent of your love? Will the description portray a woman who focused on self-care, exercising the fruits of the Spirit, has a spiritual discipline, a growth mindset, a clean heart, and is thriving in her identity?

Or would you drop it off in the dark, when your neighbor isn't home, because you are too embarrassed to look them in the eye and present them with a tattered, faded, frameless portrait, with the description of wear, worry, self-doubt, anxiety, poor health, spiritually dehydration, unforgiveness, bitterness, a fixed mindset, and barely surviving?

Which portrait would you want to receive? Be careful before you answer the question because the portrait you select is the one that portrays you as yourself. If you are satisfied with offering that gift today, you are ready to love your neighbor as yourself.

If you would be tempted to drop that gift off in the dark, there is still some work to do. A painting can be restored and brought back to life and so can you. You serve a loving Shepherd who specializes in restoration. He shows up for us when we call on Him and loves us unconditionally. In this important text, Jesus is teaching us to **show up** for ourselves first, so we can show up for others.

Show Up even if it means showing up "kicking and screaming" or even when it is hard to be kind to and forgive yourself, let go, move on, show yourself compassion, speak life into to yourself, take care of your whole self, and even pray for yourself. Like the Nike slogan, even if you don't want to, Just Show Up!

Then and only then, can you love your neighbor as yourself!

1. What are some of the best ways that you show love to your neighbor?

2. What areas do you need to start showing up for yourself?

3. How can you demonstrate that you love yourself?

NOTES:

DAY 23: MORE BEAUTIFUL THAN YOU THINK

Charm is deceitful, and beauty is passing,
But a woman who fears the Lord, she shall be praised.
Psalm 31:30

In 2013, Dove produced a short film entitled *Dove Real Beauty Sketches* as part of its marketing campaign for real beauty. The purpose of the film was to show women they are more beautiful than they think they are by comparing self-descriptions to those of strangers. In the video, several women describe themselves to a forensic sketch artist who is unable to see his subjects. The same women are then described by strangers whom they met the previous day.

What was fascinating about this experiment was what happened when the sketches were compared. Invariably, the strangers' visual images were far more flattering and more closely reflected the subject's image of themselves. When the women saw the differences, it made them quite emotional. Sadly, they didn't think they were as beautiful as they were.

This campaign was inspired by market research that suggested only 4 percent of women describe themselves as beautiful, and approximately 54 percent believe that when it comes to how they look, they are their own worst beauty critic. While this message focused on external beauty, many of the strangers described the women by features that could only come from inner beauty, such as the warmth of their smile or the brightness of their eyes.

Christian women are not immune to the trap of not feeling as beautiful as they really are. Images portrayed in social media, advertising, celebrities, and reality shows can tempt women to define beauty by the world's view instead of God's view. There is a deception all around that external beauty is more important than inner beauty. This is the world's standard. When we judge ourselves by the world's standard, we will never measure up. This can be a real barrier to thriving in our true identity.

There will always be someone skinner, or taller; with more money, a bigger house, and a better car. This deception can leave women with the constant feeling of dissatisfaction. Sadly, some women have seen their outward beauty as their only asset. It defines their self-worth and unfortunately leaves them vulnerable to the wrong intentions of men. So many women have suffered from an inferiority complex because they have who they believe is a more beautiful sister or friend, one who always seems to get all the attention.

When women base their worth and happiness on worldly standards, their souls can become paralyzed and destroyed. What we believe determines how we live. No matter what you want to achieve, the way you see yourself will govern whether you reach it or not. If you believe a lie, you act on that lie. In either case, you've made a decision based on a lie. Oftentimes that lie causes us *not* to act or **show up**.

The next time you look in the mirror and are tempted to see the flaws, or the next time you turn down an opportunity to show up and you want to shrink back, look in God's mirror, which is His Word, and affirm yourself with His truth:

Do not let your adornment be merely outward—arranging the hair, wearing gold, or putting on fine apparel—rather let it be the hidden person of the heart, with the incorruptible beauty of a gentle and quiet spirit, which is very precious in the sight of God.

1 Peter 3:3–4

But the Lord said to Samuel, "Do not look at his appearance or at the height of his stature, because I have refused him. For the Lord does not see as man sees; for man looks at the outward appearance, but the Lord looks at the heart."

1 Samuel 16:7

In like manner also, that the women adorn themselves in modest apparel, with propriety and moderation, not with braided hair or gold or pearls or costly clothing, ¹⁰but, which is proper for women professing godliness, with good works.

1 Timothy 2: 9–10

It's freeing to embrace who we are, who we were made to be. The problem occurs when we're no longer celebrating who we are when we see ourselves in the mirror, especially when we try to change ourselves. You are a masterpiece, His *Mona Lisa*. You are beautiful. God loves you. You aren't supposed to be like anyone else.

Thrive in your true identity! Accept His truth that you are more beautiful than you think you are.

"God's Masterpiece"
Ephesians 2:10

1. What do you see when you look in the mirror?

2. Who else can you help to see their true beauty?

DAY 24: SHOW UP NO MATTER WHAT

As you do not know what is the way of the wind, Or how the bones grow in the womb of her who is with child, So you do not know the works of God who makes everything.
Ecclesiastes 11:5

How do we "show up" when we are not sure how things will turn out? The synonym for "show up" is *to reveal the true nature*. Revealing our true nature (our talents, gifts, dreams,) can feel like a risk. Ecclesiastes 11 gives instruction on what it means to thrive in our true identity and show up no matter what. It advises us to cast our nets among the waters, diversify our investments, our talents.

Solomon advises to give freely. Though it may seem to be thrown away or lost, give to many. Don't make excuses for not doing what you are called to do now and in the future. It is not lost, but well laid out.

There's a story of an old golfer who could no longer see and needed someone to tell him where the ball was. Another man came to help him who could see perfectly, but when asked him where the ball landed, he couldn't remember. Moral of the story, even the best-laid plans don't always work out.

So how should we live when we are not sure how things will turn out?

Show Up and Take Risks. Don't hide because the world will not cooperate. Live confidently. Solomon implores us to not play it safe and avoid blessings because of the concerns that come with them. Are you one who will not get married because there are too many divorces? Or won't start the business because it may fold?

God wants us to step out in faith and take risks. Therefore, Solomon says, "diversify your investments." Don't put all your grain in one ship. Put your wheat in several ships, and send it out in a diversified way, so that if one ship sinks, you will not be ruined. This is similar to the popular phrase, "Don't put all your eggs in one basket."

It would be safe to not even send out your grain but keep it and make bread. But that's all you'll have. When you send grain across the sea, you take a risk. There are pirates, shipwrecks, and the unknown. You may never see your grain again. Yet there are always prospects of a dividend.

Solomon says, in Ecclesiastes 11:2 to "Give a portion to seven or eight." If you have tried every avenue there is, add one more. Why? The phrase, "You do not know," appears four times in Ecclesiastes 11:2–6. God and His work cannot be known by a fallen mankind. Do not be reckless with your investment, but don't sit on it either.

Show Up and Seize the Day. *Carpe Diem*. We cannot predict the events of our lives or control what others or nature will do (Ecclesiastes 11:6). Don't waste your time with God's affairs. "The Earth is the Lord's and the fullness thereof." Let God be God.

Do not wait for conditions to be perfect. (Ecclesiastes 11:4) Today's work may not prosper, but tomorrow's work just may. If you are a student seek to accomplish all your dreams. If you are married, don't wait for your spouse to be perfect. Pour into him now.

Do not settle for a "settle-for" Christianity. We do not know the activity of God (Ecclesiastes 11:5).   God doesn't do insider trading. He will not tell you the plan, but will tell you your duty, which is to show up, build and follow your heart. "A man's heart plans his way, But the Lord directs his steps." Proverbs 16:9.

Show Up and Sow. "In the morning, sow your seed; and in the evening, don't become idle" (Ecclesiastes 11:6). We have reason to expect evil, for we are born to trouble. But it is wise to do good in the day of prosperity.

Riches cannot profit us if we are not a blessing to others. Every man must labor to be a blessing to that place where the providence of God casts him. If we magnify every difficulty, we shall never go on.

Show up and go through with your work. Winds and tribulations are in God's hands and designed to try us. God's work shall agree with his word, whether we see it or not. And we may well trust God to provide for us. "Do not be weary in well doing for in due season, in God's time, you shall reap." Galatians 16:9.

Show up—no matter what!

1. What gifts, talents, or dreams are you hiding because the world won't cooperate?

2. What are you waiting for?

3. Where can you sow and be more of a blessing to others?

NOTES:

DAY 25: FEAR-LESS

Sarah obeyed Abraham, calling him lord,
whose daughters you are if you do good and are not afraid with any terror.
1 Peter 3:6

On March 7, 2017, a day before International Women's Day, a bronze statue of a fearless girl was placed directly in front of the iconic Wall Street charging bull in New York City. State Street Global Advisors, whose objective was to promote gender diversity and to advocate getting more women on corporate boards, commissioned the work. The work highlighted the significant role that women play in positively impacting a stronger economy and company performance.

The statue depicts a girl in a dress and sneakers, with hands on her hips and chin up. While many articles described her as the defiant girl, Kristen Visbal, creator of the bronze sculpture, commented, "I made sure to keep her features soft; she's not defiant, she's brave, proud, and strong, not belligerent." The plaque has footprints where people can stand that states: "Until she's there, stand for her. #FearlessGirl."

This plaque and statue remind us of the incredible responsibility of having a voice, using that voice, and understanding your *why*. You are wherever you are for this season for a reason. Your voice needs to be heard. In the words of Michelle Obama, "If you are scared to use your voice, then you've got to get up and give it to someone who isn't afraid to use the spot."

It takes a lot of courage to speak up when you are the only voice; whether it is in the workplace, in your family, on a church board, or wherever you are in the minority, and especially when someone tries to manipulate you to make you back down. When you are a minority speaking on behalf of a minority, you face the risk of being labeled biased or emotional (which can be synonymous for *weak*). You can then decide if you want to be a peacekeeper or a peacemaker. Many confuse the two.

A peacekeeper will maintain peace by avoiding conflict. You will recognize when you are in this place as it is; everyone else will be happy but you will likely experience inner turmoil. Throughout my life was often told from previous generations: "Don't rock the boat" and "keep the peace." Sadly, it's a subtle form of avoidance or denial. It's a mindset that keeps us in bondage, builds resentment, silences our voices, makes us shrink, and lands us right back in the cocoon.

A peacemaker, on the other hand, is willing to face and resolve conflicts to establish peace with others and within themselves. Peacemakers understand that sometimes, peace has to be lost temporarily for it to be gained. That disruption of peace means having difficult but courageous conversations so that peace can prevail. It could also mean stepping into an area where no one has dared to show up, speaking truth to bring about change, highlighting the pain in order to bring peace.

If you want to be a difference maker, you must start by being a peacemaker. Sarah, Abraham's wife, was a difference maker. First Peter 3 encourages us to be "Sarah's daughters." Sarah possessed the qualities that empower a woman to "do the right thing"—even in fearful situations. As a result, God recognized her as an example for all women to follow. The inner qualities of a gentle and quiet spirit are precious in God's sight.

To have great peace, you must have great faith. That depends on what you are feeding yourself. *It is not what you say to me that matters; it is what I say to me that matters.* Therefore, it is most important to understand "me." Sometimes you must talk back to fear! You are Sarah's daughter when you can stay calm in the midst of a chaotic situation. You are Sarah's daughter when you courageously disrupt the conversation to gain peace.

You are a peacemaker, someone who declares war on anything that disturbs your peace!

You thrive in true identity when you use your voice and your platform, wherever God has placed you, for such a time as this.

Blessed are the peacemakers, For they shall be called sons [and daughters] *of God.*
Matthew 9:5

"Until she's there, stand for her. #FearlessGirl."

1. Are you a peacekeeper or a peacemaker?

2. What is causing you inner turmoil that you need address to gain peace?

NOTES:

DAY 26: POWER OF TWO

Two are better than one, because they have a good reward for their labor. For if they fall, one will lift up his companion. But woe to him who is alone when he falls, For he has no one to help him up.
Ecclesiastes 4:9–10

It was Women's Day at my church, which meant all the Women's Season events would culminate on this day. I was the chairperson of the committee. We had experienced a mighty move of God in the first service. I was expected to lead the closing service that afternoon. I went home after the first service only to fall ill—so much so that I had no choice but to yield and call someone to replace me at the afternoon service.

About a half hour later I heard a knock at my door. A sister from the church had heard I was sick and boldly **showed up** on my doorstep to pray for me. I could barely get out of bed, but somehow made it to the door. This sister was discerning enough to know I was under spiritual attack and refused to leave me in my current state.

She declared, "You will be at the service this afternoon," and prayed over me. Instantly, I felt better and was able to lead the afternoon service.

Although this experience happened many years ago, it was a service I will never forget. Many people stopped me after the service to ask what had happened since the morning service, because they noticed such a glow about me. My sister **showed up** and prayed for me. I experienced the power of two.

Ecclesiastes 4:9 reads, "Two are better than one." The book of Ruth speaks of the significance of two and what two can do when two walk through! Amidst national unrest and personal tragedy, Ruth and Naomi developed a deep, lasting friendship that embodied God's love. David and Jonathan were two who walked through. Elizabeth and Mary were two who walked through. We all need a Ruth, an Elizabeth, a friend who will walk us through. We all need the support of a companion.

You cannot run through life. You have to walk through. On this journey, no one wants to go it alone. When you walk together with a friend, you understand the toils they have endured. You know all about the struggles, the pain, the insecurities, and the failures; and when you see from whence they came to where they are now, you can't help but share their glory and celebrate success, whatever that may look like to them. Walk through the mountains and the valleys, the sun and the storm, the pain and the promotion!

Rejoice with those who rejoice. Weep with those who weep. Show up to help your sister thrive in her true identity.

When two walk through, we strengthen each other. With a friend you can face the worst. That's the standard for a friend. Would I want this person walking with me through a bout with cancer or a painful divorce? Job loss? Physical abuse? What about a truth teller? A friend is one who, when asked for an honest opinion, will actually give it. They will say, "I think you're aiming too low," "I think you're settling," "I believe you can do this."

When you show up for your friend, you show up with honesty and accountability. Zechariah 13:6 says, "And one shall say to him, What are these wounds in your hands? Then he shall answer, Those with which I was wounded in the house of my friends."

A helpful friend will give you truth and help to build you up. They will pray for you, encourage you, believe with you, dream with you, strengthen you, and walk with you until you make it through. "Though one may be overpowered by another, two can withstand him. And a threefold cord is not quickly broken" (Ecclesiastes 4:12).

The Christian journey is a shared experience. We are not to walk alone. The apostle Paul tells us to "bear one another's burdens" (Galatians 6:2). In other words, **show up** to help or aid one another along the way.

Oh, what two can do! When two walk through, you **get** through. When two walk through, you believe you **can do.** When two walk through, you can step up, grow up, get up, look up, rise up, stand up and **show up.**

Oh, what two can do when two walk through!

1. Am I the friend that I need someone else to be?

2. Who needs me to *show up*, so that they can thrive in their true identity?

Then he said, "Take the arrows;" so he took them. And he said to the king of Israel,
"Strike the ground;" so he struck three times, and stopped. And the man of God was
angry with him, and said, "You should have struck five or six times; then you would have
struck Syria till you had destroyed it! But now you will strike Syria only three times."

2 Kings 13:18–19

One morning, while running to catch the ferry, a couple of people along the way told me not to bother, that I would never catch it, and do not waste my time. For a minute, I was tempted to turn around because I bought in to what they said. I decided however, that I would give catching the ferry my best shot and I went for it. Not only did I catch the ferry, but I had another minute to spare. If I had listened to the negative advice of those two people, I would have missed my ferry.

Sometime later, while working on my Ph.D., we had an unexpected family medical challenge, which meant that during a critical time, I wrote most of my research papers overseas from hospital rooms, cafeterias, and lounges, all while working my full time job remotely. I was blessed, however, with an incredibly supportive circle of friends within my cohort who wholeheartedly supported me and did everything they could to help me win.

I pushed hard, and surprisingly—even though I was exhausted—I managed to keep up with my assignments. I submitted one paper, however, that was not my best work. In his comments, my professor recommended that I stop, request a one-year sabbatical from the program, and start again with another cohort.

Feeling defeated, I heeded his instructions and dropped out of the cohort I loved. That one comment stopped me from trying further. Later, when I my new cohort began, I had to be on campus during my old cohort's graduation weekend. I kept asking myself, *what would have happened if I just kept going?* I **showed up,** but gave up.

In 2 King 13, King Joash approached Elisha on his deathbed for a last piece of advice, because Israel was under attack. Elisha gave Joash instructions to "strike the ground" with the arrows. Joash struck the ground three times, which made Elisha angry. For Joash had obeyed Elisha's command, but only made a half-hearted effort. Despite hearing Elisha's promise that God would bring his nation complete victory over Israel's enemies, Joash did the bare minimum. The angry Elisha told him he should have struck the ground five or six times and he would have had complete victory. *Striking the ground* means to do all you do with all your might, enthusiasm, and full commitment.

How sad it is when we go to God with our prayer concerns, He gives us instructions, then we make a half-hearted effort and are disappointed when we don't receive the victory. I have had to confess on several occasions for praying for a breakthrough and then giving up on the prayer if I don't receive it within my timeline. Showing up is not a one-time event.

Showing up means to keep striking the arrows. Even if you experience a certain degree of success just as Joash did, why settle for a portion of your blessing when can have complete victory? Showing up takes grit; we must be resilient.

Showing up also means sometimes you must pray **and** fast. You must keep striking the ground. I believe it's important to have the mindset of Jacob who said, "I won't let go until you bless me" (Genesis 32:26).

As you thrive in your true identity, there will always be someone who will try to make you give up. That person may be someone else, or it may just be you.

Let us not get in our own way of **showing up** and receive only a half victory because of our lack of passion and perseverance.

God wants you to have complete victory, receive all the promises that He has for you, and thrive in your true identity!

1. What would a victorious life look like for you?

2. Consider all the things God has called you to do. Do you do them half-heartedly or wholeheartedly? (i.e. "striking the ground" three times or five or six times?)

3. How has God been speaking to you about showing up and not giving up?

"God's Masterpiece"
Ephesians 2:10

So he commanded the chariot to stand still. And both Philip and the eunuch went down into the water, and he baptized him. Now when they came up out of the water, the Spirit of the Lord caught Philip away, so that the eunuch saw him no more; and he went on his way rejoicing.

Acts 8:38–39

While traveling from Utah to Bermuda, I stopped early in the morning for a layover in Alberta, Canada. There was no one in the airport at my gate, except for a Nigerian lady. Since I knew all the stores and restaurants in the airport would be closed, I bought some refreshments for breakfast back in Utah. I thought perhaps she had a long flight as well, so I offered her some of my refreshments. She said she had just left home in Canada and graciously accepted my offer.

We boarded our plane soon after. When we boarded the small jet plane, we discovered we were the only two people on the flight. Through the Spirit, we both knew the other was a believer. I learned her name was Rose and we talked for hours about the things of God.

Later I learned that she, a distinguished faculty at a top tier university in Canada, had just written a book. Her book was the testimony of how she painstakingly planned an escape from her household, where she was physically abused, to a homeless shelter with her five small children.

Three months after our flight, Rose came to visit Bermuda at my invitation, and we began the journey of spending weeks ministering healing to women in homeless shelters, women's shelters and fellowships, homes, and women's prisons. The women's prison was the highlight for me, as we saw many lives touched by God's Word. One lady, after giving her heart to the Lord, stood out to me. Her regal stance reminded me of that of a queen. Before we left, I quietly reminded her that she *was* a queen.

Some years later, I ran into this same woman in the city. I was elated to see her but wasn't sure if I should say anything because I wanted to honor her privacy and didn't want to remind her of her past. Before I could finish my line of self-questioning, she approached me and thanked me for speaking life to her while she was in a dark place. Imagine my surprise, then, when we a guest praise team visited our church, and *she* was one of the lead singers! Our queen! We locked eyes and smiled while I tried desperately to hold back the tears. He who the Son sets free is free indeed! (John 8:36)

Out of what seemed to be a chance encounter between two ladies came something beautiful. In Acts 8, the paths of two men crossed, but theirs was no chance encounter. It was divine providence. Philip was on his way to Gaza and an Ethiopian eunuch was on his way home. Eunuchs were men deprived of some or all their sexual organs. The angel gave instructions to Philip to travel a specific way, and the Spirit of God told Philip to go to the chariot and stay near it. At the same time, the Ethiopian eunuch was reading, but had no revelation. In his role, he was in charge of the treasury and surrounded by wealth, but he was poor in spirit (Matthew 5:3).

Despite his circumstances, the Ethiopian was a God chaser. When you are a God chaser, God will give you the revelation, even though you may not understand. Even though you might be considered by others as inferior, the Lord thinks so much of you that He will send someone to help equip you. He will empower you with His word. By His divine providence, He will set things up and put people in place so you can be in position to receive your blessing.

To some, it may have looked like this Ethiopian had no chance of receiving the revelation of salvation, but he got so much more. He asked, "Why shouldn't I be baptized?" He received understanding but wanted to go deeper. The Lord had one man, Philip, leave a revival to walk along a desert route. He came at the right time when the eunuch was studying the text. One sheep, in the shepherd's estimation, is enough to move the hand of God!

It didn't matter that this man was black. His work as a dignitary did not matter— it was what was in his heart. Ethiopia is far, but God sends His word to the ends of the earth. He would do whatever it took to find *you* too! The Ethiopian had to overcome many trials and tribulations and still persevere in the face of overwhelming odds. He did great things for Candace, the queen, but he went on to accomplish even greater things for God.

Because God was at work in his life in a providential and empowering way, the Ethiopian man maximized what he had. His position enabled him to travel to the temple. His wealth gave him access to an expensive scroll to read the Word. He grabbed hold of Philip as a teacher to baptize him. He worked with what he had, and God did the rest. There was greatness about the eunuch. But even though he was a successful figure and led a comfortable life, he was not satisfied.

One day on a journey from Jerusalem, he made a decision that granted him royal status, even greater than that of a queen; he became a son of the heavenly King. You can't activate your faith until you begin the journey! **Show Up** and you will be surprised by who God will bring and what He will do along the way. He will do it for His glory, for kingdom purposes. And it will be a butterfly effect.

The eunuch's spirit of excellence gave him access to be in a position that enabled him to go to Jerusalem to worship. His hunger for the Word gave him revelation. He read and wanted to know more. His revelation led him to the water, which sparked activation. Something came alive inside of him and left him rejoicing. He started on the journey as a eunuch and returned as a king. Now he knew who he was, what his real privileges and rights were, the treasures he had access to, and the word of God and His promises: greater life and greater love.

God will send someone to your chariot. The eunuch didn't let castration emasculate him. When others saw him as a eunuch, God saw him as a king. He was trapped, but the Lord activated his royalty and gave him access to the real treasury. He no longer had to search for who He was. Luke 17:21 says, "nor will they say, 'See here!' or 'See there!' For indeed, the kingdom of God is within you."

"But you are a chosen generation, a royal priesthood, a holy nation, His own special people, that you may proclaim the praises of Him who called you out of darkness into His marvelous light" (1 Peter 2:9)..

1. What access has God granted you that you can leverage?

2. What will you do to show up and start your journey?

3. In what ways will you embrace your inner queen?

PART
5

Powttering Up

DAY 29: FUEL UP

Then he said, "Go, borrow vessels from everywhere, from all your neighbors—empty vessels; do not gather just a few. And when you have come in, you shall shut the door behind you and your sons; then pour it into all those vessels and set aside the full ones." So she went from him and shut the door behind her and her sons, who brought the vessels to her; and she poured it out.

2 Kings 4:3–5

Today is the first day of **PowHering Up,** and we are in the fueling zone. Some months ago, I arrived home late and delayed getting gas until the morning because I was tired. The next morning, focused on my destination, I forgot to get gas before I began my journey. I remembered about five miles from the city, traffic came to a complete standstill.

I crawled for one hour, until to my horror, I saw my gas gauge turn to empty. I had at least another hour's journey into the city, or to any gas station, but I could not go forward, only go backward.

In self-inflicted frustration, I made a U-turn to head back to a gas station, and you guessed it…I started my two-hour journey all over again.

Has that ever happened in your life? You knew there was a risk of your oil running low, and yet you delayed your decision to be filled? A crisis came along, and you had to get an emergency supply and start your journey all over again.

Oil in Scripture is symbolic of the Holy Spirit. God has caused the oil of His Spirit to reside in these earthen vessels; these clay pots that are our lives. How full is your vessel? Are you running on empty?

While running on empty in the literal sense means out of fuel, the phrase's definition has many parallels to our spiritual walk.

First, we can appear to be full, but in reality are empty or on automatic pilot, and continue to show up in church, attend women's fellowship, say all the right Christian phrases, but going through the motions. You may have lost all joy, appearing full, but in a dry and thirsty place, no longer feeling his presence.

You may be half empty, losing enthusiasm. The oil is not all gone, but you are oscillating between doing these things in your own strength, trying to do life your way and when that doesn't work, switch to God's way; seeing God as a backup source.

Lastly, you may be empty, at the end of your resources, at a level of oil that is inadequate to sustain you. Life has drained you. The burdens of life have sucked all the oil from you and you are not in place. You are "sitting at a neighbor's house", empty, a place that is not your dwelling place, and you need to be rescued.

If you recognize that you are at that place, appearing full but half empty, half empty or empty, your vessel needs to be filled. Allow God to show you where you are on the gauge. You might have to make a U-turn and start your journey all over again.

God is gracious. You might say, "I'm not sure where to begin." Here are three considerations to get you started on your journey.

1. **Go back to Goshen**. Oftentimes, circumstances can shake your vessel and turn it into a marred or broken vessel. No matter what the circumstances are, the Lord desires to take you from the neighbor's house and bring you back to Goshen. The meaning of Goshen is *to draw near*. James 4:8 says, "Draw near to God and he will draw near to you."

2. **Get back on the Potter's Wheel**. Arise, go down to the potter's house (Isaiah 64:8). As clay vessels, each of us must take a journey. The steps in this journey can be painful, but they are necessary for transforming us from broken bits of clay into anointed vessels that reflect the glory of God.

   When the Master Potter first finds you in the field, you might be a broken vessel, frustrated and in need of healing. But the Potter takes a rock and pounds your broken pieces into fine dust. As you cry out, He lets you know that He's simply removing all the debris (resentment, bitterness, anger, unforgiveness, pride) from our lives so He can moisten us and put us back on the potter's wheel.

He then applies the heat. As we cry out, He shapes us and molds us, forming us into the vessel He purposed us to be. And then, proudly, He puts us back on the shelf, fit for the Master's use. The Potter wants to put you back together again.

3. **Let God fill you up**. It is God who fills His vessel with the treasure of His Word. As our Lord said unto the Samaritan woman at the well, "If thou will notice the gift of God and who it is that said to thee, 'Give me to drink' thou wouldst have asked of him and he would have given the living water," (John 4:10). God wants to fill you up so you can be poured out. As He pours you out into empty vessels, you keep getting fueled up.

Take the little God has given to you and allow Him to use it for His glory and to pour you out as you thrive in your true identity! You will be filled beyond measure as you Fuel up and PowHer up to PowHer share!

1. Are you running on empty?

2. In what ways can you "go back to Goshen" and draw near to God?

3. What debris needs to be removed on the Potter's Wheel?

4. What do you need to do to be filled?

> And Barak said to her, "If you will go with me, then I will go; but if you will not go with me, I will not go!" So she said, "I will surely go with you; nevertheless there will be no glory for you in the journey you are taking, for the LORD will sell Sisera into the hand of a woman."
>
> Judges 4:9

"You're not sorry." Those were the words spoken to me by an elderly lady at a women's conference I attended many years ago. Each night of the conference, I was careful to sit on the end of the row, so I could leave quickly and avoid the crowds in the massive stadium. One night, however, the usher put me right in the middle of the row and I had no choice but to stay planted. Of course, that one night was the first time I had to use the restroom in the middle of the service.

As I climbed over the many other ladies in the row, I apologized profusely upon leaving and returning. After the service, an elderly lady from my row asked if she could speak with me. She held me by both my hands, looked me in the eye and said firmly, "You are not sorry."

It took me a minute to process her words. At first I thought she meant I really wasn't sorry, that I was purposely rude by climbing over everyone in my row multiple times, but as she repeated herself, I realized her deeper message: "Do not be sorry." In other words, stop apologizing when no apology is necessary!

Women are known for over-apologizing. A woman's tendency to over-apologize, however, fosters a passive mindset and inhibits our ability to thrive in our true identity. Over-apologizing is a confidence killer and diminishes a woman's powHer. Consider the number of times yesterday you said "sorry." "Sorry, I just have one more question;" "Sorry, do you have a minute?" or "I may be wrong, but…"

Many women were raised to put a higher value on empathy than on strength; therefore, when situations call for strength, they are often preceded with an apology. When women over-apologize with their words and actions, they insinuate that they do not belong. Too often, women worry about hurting people's feelings and causing offense.

This was not the case with Deborah, the judge and prophetess, when she gave Barak instructions on how to win the war; but he refused to go without her. Deborah was then *not sorry* when she told him the war would be won by the hand of a woman. She was a woman of great strength and she did not mince her words. She had to deliver a stern word to Barak when she told him he would not get the glory (Judges 4:9). While it may have been hurtful to hear, she spoke truth and made no apology for it. Deborah was direct. She knew her true identity and walked in it.

Deborah was confident about the word God had given her, and she delivered it with courage. Since God told Deborah what to say, she became the go-to person for the settling of conflicts between others. People knew Deborah only spoke words the Lord gave to her. This quality built her credibility as a leader. She was a model of how to balance empathy with strength.

Apologies have become the language of a peacekeeper. They make us shrink by minimizing our presence and value. It's hard to powHer Up when you are PowHering down.

Apologizing when you have done something wrong is a strength and is necessary, but apologizing when you have done nothing wrong is a sign of weakness. It's time to stop apologizing and start harnessing the powHer of your voice!

Consider the closing words of Deborah, the great warrior-prophetess of Israel:

Thus let all Your enemies perish, O Lord!
But let those who love Him be like the sun when it comes out in full strength.
(Judges 5:31)

PowHerful women, let our words and actions not be dimmed by unnecessary apologies that make us weak.

Let us PowHer up and shine like the sun when it comes out in full strength!

Oh, and one more thing, if my strength makes you uncomfortable…I make no apology!

1. In what situations do I find myself over-apologizing?

2. Would anyone say this about my qualities: "like the sun when it comes out in full strength"?

3. What can I do to change my mindset and rise up in strength?

_____

_____

_____

_____

_____

_____

_____

_____

DAY 31: POWHER UP

For by You I can run against a troop,
By my God I can leap over a wall.
Psalm 18:29

Today is the final day of our 31-Day Bible Study challenge. We have been empowHered by the Word and are ready to PowHer up. Today is also the first time my computer will not "power up." I am, therefore, writing this final devotion on my phone. I will not be discouraged because I know I am connected to a higher Power source, and so are *you*!

Because we are God's masterpieces and are connected to the chief Power source, we are unstoppable.

The mountains of identity may be steep. But we have hind's feet. Navigating life through "in" groups and "out" groups, is enough to make you weary. One day you can be surrounded by your "in" group of family, friends, sisters, and brothers in Christ, who propel you to fly and spread your wings. You are secure in who you are because you are embraced, celebrated, and your strengths are activated.

The next day you might be in a foreign place where you are frustrated, the only person in the "out" group, where your gifts could be castrated. *Misunderstood* may be an understatement when you factor in the layers of cultural, gender, and other areas of your identity that make you different. These are your mountains.

You want to thrive, but you have been doing everything just to survive. In some others' minds, your identity alone may disqualify you. Be sure, however, that *you* don't disqualify you.

There may not be an expectation that you will win. You may have been labeled several things for a number of reasons. These are your troops. It's not what they call you; it's what you answer to!

The life decisions we make are based on how we see ourselves. What you accept or reject all depends on what you reflect. The declaration of your identity will determine your destiny.

We are accountable for what we know. Now that you know your location, (where you stand in God's eyes), your position should have changed. You now have the PowHer to use your voice, go for your dreams, change your language, overcome fear, answer your calling, and walk away from anything or anyone who powers you down.

While the mountain of self-limiting beliefs, negative self-talk, low self-esteem, and failures may be high, and the troop of glass ceilings, those who have spoken against you, abused you, didn't choose you, left you, and betrayed you may be many, you can still thrive! With God's help, you can run against that troop and you can leap over that mountain (Psalm 18:29).

PowHerful lady, you are free to thrive in your true identity! "Stand fast therefore in the liberty by which Christ has made us free, and do not be entangled again with a yoke of bondage" (Galatians 5:1).

Declare with me: "Dear future, I'm ready to make that leap!"

Arise, God's Masterpiece, and PowHer up for the next leg of the journey!

1. What are your mountains?

2. What are your troops?

3. Are you ready to make the leap?

Now faith is the substance of things hoped for,
the evidence of things not seen.
Hebrews 11:1

EPILOGUE

You did it! You stayed the course. You were intentional about thriving in your identity for 31 days! I pray that you have been positively impacted and ready to powHer up and be all that God has called you to be!

The topic of identity is complex and yet so important. Every decision we make depends on how we see ourselves, what we think we deserve, how we see our worth and the things we accept. In these times of fear and uncertainty, one thing is constant, our identity in Christ. Knowing who you are is more critical now than ever. Everyday your identity will be challenged. That means that, like a butterfly, you may have to rise from the cocoon and journey through the uncomfortable growth phase of shedding some old beliefs, habits, thinking, or even friends, in order to experience the beauty of the glow up. You have it in you. You are stronger and more beautiful than you think you are.

It's time to show up and soar. Show up for yourself and others. Embrace what God's word says about you and allow it to manifest in your life. There are great treasures inside of you. It is time to uncover what is hidden and rediscover your authentic self

You have a choice to show up as your authentic self or 'play it safe' and hide the real you, continuing to conform but staying dissatisfied. The decision should be easy, but rather it is one of the greatest struggles, particularly for women. Yes, the call to powHer up can be overwhelming but *you cannot shrink and hide your way to greatness*. It's time to *Thrive in your True Identity*!

ABOUT THE AUTHOR

Dr. Crystal Clay is the Founder of Olive Branch Consulting International, a Coaching and Leadership Development Company that supports clients' efforts to reinvent, reposition or rediscover themselves for maximum meaningful impact. Dr. Crystal Clay is an Executive Coach and Gallup Strengths Coach. She has coached hundreds of women from various countries.

Her expertise builds upon her experience as a Talent Development Leader in global organisations, a Certified Diversity and Inclusion Facilitator through Harvard University's Conflict Management Group and her PhD in Organisational Leadership from Regent University.

Crystal is dedicated to supporting the community and has spent several years serving as Director on Education Boards and in ministry leadership roles. She is a facilitator and speaker for charities, faith-based, and women's events, team building and strategic planning retreats.

Through grit, resilience and a passion for life-long learning, Crystal has used every decade of her life to take on new challenges and reinvent herself in some way. When she celebrated her last decade, she took on the challenge of reinventing herself and became a business owner.

Crystal is now here to extend the "Olive Branch" to help women seeking a fresh start by reinventing themselves to expand their influence and make a meaningful impact.

If you are ready to *Thrive* but could benefit from peer encouragement or want to know more about our events, resources or speaking engagements:

Join our thriving Facebook community: Thrive in True Identity

Follow us on Instagram: @drcrystalclay

Website: www.drcrystalclay.com or www.olivebranch.bm

Email: info@drcrystalclay.com

To receive a free copy of the e-book, *Reinvent You,* go to www.drcrystalclay.com.

www.ingramcontent.com/pod-product-compliance
Lightning Source LLC
Chambersburg PA
CBHW021143090426
42740CB00008B/907